Playful Learning

Playful Learning

Develop Your Child's Sense of Joy and Wonder

Text and photography by

Mariah Bruehl

ROOST
BOOKS

Boston

2011

Roost Books
An imprint of Shambhala Publications, Inc.
Horticultural Hall
300 Massachusetts Avenue
Boston, Massachusetts 02115
roostbooks.com

9 8 7 6 5 4

Printed in Malaysia

♾ This edition is printed on acid-free paper that meets the
American National Standards Institute z39.48 Standard.

♻ Shambhala Publications makes every effort to print on
recycled paper. For more information please visit www
.shambhala.com.

Distributed in the United States by Random House, Inc.,
and in Canada by Random House of Canada Ltd

Interior design and composition by Greta D. Sibley

Library of Congress Cataloging-in-Publication
Bruehl, Mariah.
Playful Learning: developing your child's sense of joy and
wonder / Mariah Bruehl.
p. cm.
ISBN 978-1-59030-819-6 (pbk.: alk. paper)
1. Learning. 2. Play. 3. Creative ability in children. I. Title.
LB1060.B775 2011
155.4'1315—dc22
2010040229

This book is dedicated to Marilyn, Ella, and every child I have ever taught, who, although they do not know it, always have been and always will be my greatest teachers.

Contents

Acknowledgments

A HEARTFELT THANKS goes to:

Shambhala Publications for publishing such a wonderful collection of books and for allowing me to share my experiences with families everywhere.

Jennifer Urban-Brown, who has given me insight into myself as a writer and has been a wonderful guide throughout the publication process.

George Nicholson and Erica Rand Silverman, whose wise advice was most helpful and reassuring.

The incredible educators who have made a profound impact on both the field of education and my own personal view of teaching and learning. The work of Maria Montessori, Loris Malaguzzi, and Howard Gardner has deeply influenced my view of children and the potential they hold.

The amazing mentors I have had the opportunity to work with over the years, to whom I will forever be grateful for the insight and experience I have gained through my time spent with them—Robert Blodget, the late Bette Jean Tryon, Debbie Reilly, Karen Katz, Stan Chu, the late Janet Stork, and Courtney Sale Ross.

My family, both near and far, who have always made me believe that anything is possible.

My parents, who have always given me the love, time, and resources that I have needed to learn, grow, and thrive.

Marilyn and Ella, who are full of wonder, insight, and love. You are my truest sources of inspiration.

Edward, who has unwaveringly loved and supported me through thick and thin. Thank you for being an amazing father, husband, friend, and my eternal rock.

This book is a compilation of my favorite educational philosophies, frameworks, curriculums, and classroom lessons. My inspiration stems from a multitude of incredible people and resources—for their work, insight, and experience I am eternally grateful. I would like to acknowledge the following people, who have been of particular inspiration to the learning experiences in this book: Lucy Calkins, Georgia Heard, Wendy Ewald, Stephanie Harvey, Anne Goudvis, Carmen McGuinness, Geoffrey McGuinness, Marilyn Burns, Mary Baratta-Lorton, Stephanie Bearce, Joni Chancer, Gina Rester-Zodrow, Joseph Cornell, Ann Pelo, MaryAnn F. Kohl, Carol Sabbeth, David Sobel, Barbara Taylor, Ken Breeding, Jane Harrison, Linda Lantiera, and Judith Anne Rice. May this book be a vehicle for helping to spread their work.

Playful Learning

Introduction

FOR AS LONG AS I CAN REMEMBER, my dream was to start a school. During my college years I became convinced that the best way to "save the world" was through education and that if I could participate in building an educational model that helped children reach their fullest potential, we would no longer struggle with many of today's societal problems. Throughout my undergraduate and graduate studies I researched, observed, and practiced many different educational theories in pursuit of discovering the best practices in the field. While teaching in the classroom, I witnessed firsthand how much an innovative and thoughtful curriculum could contribute to the lives of children.

Around the time that I became pregnant with my first child, the opportunity for me to help start a new school came to fruition. It really was a dream come true, and I believed that if the school provided my child with a world-class education, she would have all she needed to be successful in life. I was very fortunate in having the opportunity to work with brilliant teachers and educators while creating an early childhood and elementary school that I felt was one of the most innovative in the country.

A couple of years later I gave birth to my second child. While I was implementing curriculum, hiring and training teachers, and designing classrooms, I thought that I was providing the best for my daughters by working hard to create a wonderful school for them. Yet, over time I realized that my intentions were a bit (well, way) off base. The more successful I became in my career, the less time I was able to spend with my own children. Ultimately, although the girls were attending a great school, they did not have me—the support they needed at home—and they were not thriving in the ways they should have been. I thought that I could design the perfect curriculum to be taught in classrooms, for my own children and for children throughout the world. Yet what I saw when looking into my young daughters' eyes is that the curriculum of life, as experienced by children in their homes on a daily basis, is the most revolutionary teaching and learning that can take place. The big hard lesson for me was that although good schools are a vital aspect of children's development, they are simply not enough.

The family—whatever shape, form, or construct it may take—is the most important aspect of a child's life. I was putting my heart and soul into what I thought were the big and important things, and did not realize that for children, it is the small things that make the greatest difference. It was this realization that inspired me to make a major shift in my life. Rather than placing all my energy into developing schools, I shifted my focus to nurturing my own family and, in turn, helping other families do the same.

Children are natural scientists, artists, mathematicians, authors, and scholars. From the time they are born they seek out information about the world around them in an effort to construct meaning and further their development. Whether they are stacking blocks for the first time or taking in new textures, sights, and sounds, children have an inherent drive to learn and make sense of their reality. When given an enriching environment and supportive guidance, they intuitively take advantage of the prospects for learning that are put before them. Current research demonstrates that children learn most effectively when they are actively engaged and enjoying themselves.[1] Ironically, many of the conditions deemed most desirable for learning can more readily be practiced at home than in school.

With this in mind, I set out to supplement my daughters' education by providing experiences for them that are sometimes difficult to achieve in classroom settings. I was excited about having the time and space to follow their personal interests and engage in meaningful activities in our own home or neighborhood, where my children are most comfortable.

However, I soon learned that moving from full-time educator to full-time mom wasn't as easy as I thought it would be. As a teacher, my focus was on creating schedules and keeping children engaged and productive throughout the day, so my first inclination was to do the same thing for my children at home. Big mistake! The girls certainly did not want to hear that it was now time to write in their writer's notebooks or that at one o'clock we would be doing a science experiment. And yes, I did try this approach! My first couple of attempts at nurturing their love of learning failed miserably. The girls were not interested in participating in my predetermined "fun activities," and I quickly became discouraged. They didn't want to be ruled by my schedule, and they had an altogether different view of what it meant to be productive. I had to slow down and tune into their rhythms. I found that I needed to put my agenda aside and just *be* with my daughters. I discovered that it was in those moments of *being* together that the opportunities for learning presented themselves.

What I eventually learned was that if I could meld my children's sense of joy and wonder with learning experiences that I had thoughtfully planned, many wonderful things occurred: my children were interested, we had fun together, and we developed a new love of learning as a family.

With this breakthrough I was encouraged to continue. The collection of activities in this book is the result of plenty of research and much trial and error. Here you will learn many ideas for enriching your child's education—all through fun projects that will engage your child's sense of wonder and imagination through hands-on experiences.

The Benefits of Playful Learning

You might ask, why go through all of this? Why not leave education in the hands of educational institutions? Well, these are great questions. As I have embarked on this journey I have enjoyed a number of unexpected benefits.

A Rewarding Family Dynamic

By participating in learning experiences with your child, not only will you be more proactive in his education, it will add a new layer to your relationship with him. The discussions that take place, the projects we engage in, the interests we share, and the things we get really excited about have all become a part of our family culture. At this point the girls see learning as a family activity and will often approach my husband and me with prospects for new projects or educational adventures. Practicing Playful Learning is not just about helping your children to become "smarter," it is about creating a family dynamic where learning is a joyful pursuit, something that will last for a lifetime.

Confident and Independent Children

When children embark on Playful Learning adventures, they develop habits of heart and mind that will stay with them throughout their lives. When your child is encouraged to wonder about the world around her and then realizes that she is capable of discovering the answers to her questions, it builds a sense of accomplishment, which leads to an independent and confident person.

My girls have a new bravado in their step and determination in their voice since becoming comfortable taking intellectual and emotional risks. Through our shared experiences they are learning that their questions are important, that their interests are worth pursuing, and that with persistence they can achieve anything they set their minds to. They now welcome challenges and independently seek out opportunities for discovery. It is also a delight to see how Playful Learning has become a part of their independent play. The girls will often emerge after a period of play with a book they have written or an enriching project they have developed together. Do they still have moments of self-doubt? The answer is a resounding yes! But we now have a repertoire of experiences to draw on and discuss, which demonstrate how perseverance pays off.

Stronger Home-School Connection

When parents share in different types of learning experiences with their children, they are able to witness firsthand their child's individual learning style and abilities. This insight helps to facilitate more meaningful communication between home and school. Another added benefit is that having a foundation of shared experiences with your child opens up the way you talk about school within your family. Engaging in Playful Learning at home has dramatically changed the way that we talk about "what happened at school." The girls come home excited to talk about connections they made at school and how they relate to what we have done together at home. When my oldest daughter starts a new writing unit at school, she comes home excited about sharing her topics of choice and will often flip through the notebook she keeps at home for more ideas. I also have a better grasp of where they are academically, because we do a lot of reading, writing, and learning together. I come to parent-teacher conferences better prepared to ask questions and engage in a meaningful dialogue about my children's development. I feel empowered because I know that I can help address any areas of school-related weakness or growth. I am more of an equal partner with their teachers, rather than a bystander hoping that the girls are getting everything they need.

A Return to Wonder

Playful Learning gives us as parents an opportunity (and excuse) to play again! It is wonderful to teach the way we wish we had been taught.

I have rediscovered my own awe and wonder of the world. Playful Learning is infectious, and I often find myself learning side by side with the girls. What started out as a mission to educate them has evolved into a collaborative inquiry into the world at large. While I have always found their enthusiasm to be contagious, I also have had the privilege of seeing the girls be inspired by my genuine delight in a new discovery. I love going through my days open to new opportunities for learning. I have developed a new pair of rose-colored glasses. Yet the lenses I am looking through do not see into a dream world; rather, they peer deeply into the world of reality and all the potential that lies within everyday things. I am thankful to have reawakened this fresh perspective (at my age!) and even more grateful that I am doing everything I can to preserve it within my own children.

To engage in the learning process with your children and to build a culture within your family that celebrates learning is one of the most honorable and rewarding endeavors you can embark upon. Schools play an important role in a child's development, but family will always be the guiding force in a child's life. My hope is that this book helps spark a love of learning for your family that will stay with you for years to come.

How to Use *Playful Learning*

WITH THE RIGHT INFORMATION and some simple tools, parents are perfectly poised to bring out the best in their children, and in the process make the world a better place for generations to come. So how do you begin? This book presents fifty-eight learning experiences in seven subject areas. These learning experiences are meant to be used organically, as interest arises from your children. I would recommend skimming this book first, so you have a collection of possible activities in the back of your mind. You will be amazed at how these ideas come back to you at just the right moment. I would also encourage you to let your children look through this book and place sticky notes on pages that feature activities that appeal to them. Nothing makes for a better experience than when the idea or desire for it comes from your child.

Once you and your child have skimmed through the book, you can refer back to it when your child becomes curious about a particular subject. For example, if your child becomes fascinated with collecting leaves, you may want to stock up on the supplies for making wire leaves. The goal of this book is not to complete each activity one by one—it is to take your child's questions and interests to the next level through meaningful experiences. My hope is that you make these projects your own and adapt them to meet the needs and interests of your children.

Teaching for Understanding

With a little bit of information and forethought, you can play a pivotal role in your children's cognitive and creative development. This isn't to say, however, that you should be giving your child quizzes to see whether they are retaining the information or facts that you're learning together. The learning experiences in this book are based on one of my greatest educational influences, a framework called Teaching for Understanding, which comes from the Harvard Graduate School of Education's Project Zero. The simplified premise of this framework is the notion that education should strive toward developing *understanding* rather than simply retaining information related to specific topics and subjects. So what does it mean to develop understanding? When a child truly understands a topic, she can ask relevant questions, make connections to real-world situations, think of new ways to use and apply the information, and transfer her knowledge to a variety of situations.[2] Understanding is a long-term goal that contains many different levels of knowledge on any given topic.

The goal of developing understanding within our children may seem lofty and elusive at times, yet it is actually a perfect fit for experiences shared at home. Parents have the freedom to spend as long as a child wants on topics that are relevant to his life and passions. We also have the ability to put a topic to rest temporarily and then return to it again days, weeks, months, or even years later when the interest is ripe. As parents, we know our children better than anyone, and we can use that insight to introduce information in ways that are exciting to them. We have a wonderful opportunity to make connections between the things that our children are interested in or currently learning about and a variety of real-world situations. We can help to make these connections explicit for our young children and watch how in turn they start to make them on their own.

With developing understanding being a long-term goal, it takes the pressure off of us to teach our children specific facts. Although I do introduce my girls to scientific names of things in many of our activities together, I do not get caught up in whether they retain them in the short term. I much prefer that after dissecting a flower, they joyfully tell their father about the reproductive cycle in their own words when he comes home from work. Their enthusiasm and desire to dissect, compare, and contrast numerous types of flowers naturally create the opportunity for internalizing and remembering the correct names over time. It is the quality of an activity that is most important and that will sustain their interest in any given topic.

Although children can learn many things from the projects listed in this book, it is helpful to keep in mind four primary goals: (1) strengthening your relationship with your children, (2) practicing and encouraging a disposition toward learning, (3) developing long-term understanding, and (4) sustaining focus on any given activity or subject for longer and longer periods of time. Facts, figures, and specific skills will all follow from meaningful experiences in which children are able to act on their curiosity, access relevant information, and enjoy the rewards that come from asking good questions and uncovering the answers.

Ingredients for Success

With this general understanding of how to approach the activities in this book, what more can you do to ensure success? Here are some things that I learned along the way.

Planning and Preparation

Thoughtful planning and preparation are important elements for participating in the learning process with your children, but they do not need to be daunting. I have often found myself suffering from "analysis paralysis" as I try to determine just the right way to present a certain topic to the girls or search for just the right supplies to use. My advice is to spend some time organizing a space that is conducive to engaging in projects (see "Playful Learning Spaces"), slowly build a collection of books and materials that are in line with the type of learning you and your children are interested in, flip through the activities and resources listed in this book, listen to and observe your children in action, and then seize the moment when you recognize that glimmer of enthusiasm coming from your child. Don't be afraid to fail and don't set your expectations too high.

As long as your shared experiences are joyful and honor your child's interests, the number of facts she learns is not important. Keep the long-term view of your child's development in mind and have fun!

Flexibility

Learning to be flexible was the most difficult aspect of this process for me. After having shopped for materials, done some research, and checked out just the right books from the library, I would be filled with images of the perfect crafty Saturday afternoon. However the girls would often have a different image of the ideal Saturday. I have learned that these moments of my own disequilibrium are make-it-or-break-it moments. If in these moments I try to push or persuade even a little, the girls can easily lose interest in "my project" forever; it instantly becomes "my thing" and not theirs. Yet if I follow their lead and find peace in the fact that when they are ready I have everything I need, we enjoy the activity when they eventually ask to partake in it on their own. I have found that my children are radars for manipulation, and if they detect that I am trying to push forward my own agenda, without taking into account what they want or need in that moment, I may as well kiss my "wonderfully inspiring" activity good-bye. The good news is that in my attempt to follow my children's interests first, I have learned a lot about them. I am now able to more accurately plan for projects that pique their interests. We have also become much closer as I have made an effort to follow their rhythms rather than impose mine upon them. The more I show respect for their interests, desires, and daily patterns of being, the more open they become to my offerings and contributions.

Spontaneity

Spontaneity and flexibility go hand in hand. I wish a had a nickel for every time that I had a great mapping project prepared, only to have the girls come running in from playing outside, excited about doing drawings of the patterns they discovered on leaves. Their enthusiasm about leaves is wonderful news, though it means that I have to quickly switch gears and reorganize a bit. It is these outbursts of enthusiasm that we as parents really want to be ready for, because they become the most memorable experiences for our children. With a little organization it is not too difficult to quickly put away the maps and take out the colored pencils, magnifying glasses, and drawing paper. Being spontaneous encourages a child's fascination with something at any given time. Now, I don't want to paint a picture that portrays me spending all day every day waiting for my children to show a spark of interest in something and then me racing around to provide them with deep and meaningful experiences; we all know that is not realistic. I do, though, make an effort to be present with them during the times we are together. A willingness to listen and then act on what you hear from your child is the type of spontaneity that is called for here.

To be spontaneous, it helps to have a few projects prepared that you can turn to when the time is right. I call this being one step ahead, which I'll discuss more later. Often you can use time during an actual activity— once your child is engaged—to find materials or do some quick research that will bring a bit more depth of understanding. If your child gleans a single new connection, insight, or fact from his work, it becomes a foundation for further inquiry and also creates a shared vocabulary that can be built upon. By honoring your child's initial excitement about a new interest and helping him pursue it, he can begin to see the world as full of learning opportunities and delight in sharing and expanding upon his discoveries with you.

Free and Unstructured Time

The importance of free and unstructured time in children's lives took me by surprise. Having worked as a teacher and administrator for so many years, I had become a master scheduler, and the idea of planning unscheduled time was a big shift for me. On the same note, I learned quickly that if I had the girls scheduled at different classes, camps, and playdates every day, they were too tired when they came home to engage in any valuable family activities. After I cleared out some time in our schedule, I realized that our most creative and productive projects came about on the days that were left wide open. It was during these relaxed afternoons or long mornings that the girls would ask about the "ant experiment" I had mentioned the previous week or would flip through a cookbook and ask to cook a certain recipe. It has also become apparent that they are learning how to navigate their own time and are making good decisions about the activities they choose for themselves. As a result, the girls are engaging in longer periods of independent play and will often head up their own investigations and projects.

Resources for Learning

In each chapter and learning experience, I have supplied you with information, ideas, and resources that will facilitate positive shared experiences with your child. Below is an overview of the different components within this book and an explanation of how they can be best utilized.

Developmental Overview

For all seven subjects presented in this book, I have written a brief developmental overview, which describes the learning stages a child goes through for that discipline. In general the overviews describe the typical developmental process for children approximately three to eight years old. With that said, it is important to note that every child is unique and each discipline entails a different path of development. My hope is that parents do not spend much time focusing on what skills their child is exhibiting at a particular age, but rather identify where their child is currently within the continuum of learning and help to successfully move him forward from that point.

The One-Step-Ahead Parent: Teaching What We Don't Understand

With the goal of developing understanding within our children, we must understand various subjects ourselves; however, we don't need to be experts on any given subject. A great teacher once told me that in order to start teaching young children a new topic, we simply need to be a few children's books ahead of our students. I like to call this phenomenon the "one step ahead" parent.

Now I really do mean that parents simply need to be just one step ahead of any learning experience. I have been known to read a book aloud on a topic on the way to a museum or while at the beach—talk about one step ahead! Yet that little bit of preparation makes the difference between an ordinary experience and a learning experience.

I must admit that the girls occasionally take on spontaneous interests in topics that I know nothing about. During these times, I encourage their curiosity and may even generate a few questions myself (which is great for modeling the scientific method). Later, the process of fact-finding and researching the answers to our questions becomes the experience itself. These moments allow me to model using books and other resources to find specific information, and to demonstrate first-hand that learning truly is a lifelong endeavor. Now the girls often conduct their own research, and they love to teach their father and me about all the exciting revelations they discover. They have become our greatest teachers.

For each activity listed in this book, I have provided a section called "One Step Ahead" to provide you with facts, thoughts, or preparations that will help you to take that *one step,* which makes for a more meaningful time together.

Materials and Printables

Although many of the learning experiences in this book can be adapted to use the materials you have at home, many of them do require some preparation. I have made this as easy as possible by providing lists of the specific materials you will need and all of the relevant "printables" (which need to be printed) for each activity. The printables can be copied straight from the book or printed from the Playful Learning Web site (playful learning.net).

I like to relate each activity to a recipe from a cookbook. If you would like to prepare a recipe for a special occasion, it is important to make a list and get everything you need beforehand. The same is true for the activities in this book. A little preparation makes for a wonderful outcome!

Books to Inspire

Every learning experience can be enhanced with quality children's literature. For each project I have recommended books to inspire and enhance your Playful Learning experiences. Reading a book aloud is a wonderful way of introducing many of the activities in this book. Often when I am unsure how to introduce a project to the girls, a good picture book creates just the excitement I was hoping for.

More to Explore

In the "More to Explore" sections I have provided you with ideas on how to extend each learning experience. Pick up on your child's cues. If he shows interest in an activity, try the suggestions in this section to take your child's learning even further in the moment or at a later date.

As parents we have the benefit of taking the long-term view with our children. We plant seeds in their hearts and minds that may take weeks, months, or even years to blossom. The extraordinary thing is that the moment a seed begins to sprout within them, we can be there to help them nurture and expand upon their interest. The world is a wondrous place and is filled with awe-inspiring objects and occurrences—a grain of sand, the veins on a leaf, ants on the sidewalk, the phases of the moon, the list goes on. Let the universe be your curriculum, and you will be amazed at how many teachable moments present themselves. My wish for the world is that families embrace every opportunity they have to learn, discover, process, discuss, and experience life's big (and little) questions and challenges with their children. I promise we will all walk away better people for it.

Playful Learning Spaces

WHILE ENGAGING in learning experiences provides great opportunities for you and your child to learn and grow together, there is nothing that fosters independence and inspires creativity within children more than a thoughtfully prepared environment. While working as both a teacher and an administrator, I was profoundly aware of how the physical environment shapes children's behavior. In my own experience with designing classrooms, I have witnessed firsthand how thoughtful design can influence children's ability to learn. Every decision about presentation, organization, and selection of materials will have an impact on how children interact with their surroundings. The same principles hold true for the home. I am sure that many of you have observed how your children engage with different toys in different ways after their play areas have been cleaned up or organized. By applying the principles of good classroom design to your home, you can open up new avenues of exploration for your children, foster independence, and nurture self-esteem—and maybe even gain some precious time for yourself in the process.

When designing a space for children, it is helpful to think about the characteristics that you as an adult would like and then balance that with what your child would enjoy. Often grown-ups create spaces for children with preconceived ideas of what children like, rather than considering basic elements of what is useful and practical for them. A well-prepared environment can result in many hours of self-guided, independent, creative, and productive time for your children. Although it takes some thought and preparation, the results will be well worth it for both you and your child.

Here are questions to consider when designing spaces that inspire Playful Learning:

- Can your child access the materials in the play space independently? Are they organized in baskets or bins that are clearly labeled so your child knows how and where to put things away when finished with them?

- Are the materials presented in an attractive manner that invites your child to use them?

- Do the materials, toys, and games represent a balance between your child's and your own preferences? Do they represent what you value and thus encourage your child to engage in activities that you feel good about?

- What is your child currently interested in? If your child no longer plays with dinosaurs, but has been talking a lot about birds, make sure that the play space reflects this current passion. Rotating toys is a great way to keep your child interested in play space activities and ultimately prolongs the life of your child's playthings. It never ceases to amaze me how excited my girls get about a toy that comes back into rotation. The nostalgia they feel toward a toy they have not seen in a while is almost more than their delight over a brand-new toy.

- Is the play space a calming environment that allows one to focus on the task at hand without distracting colors, decorations, or objects?

- Are you seeing things from your child's perspective? Put yourself in your child's shoes to determine the right height for displaying and storing materials and hanging art.

- Is this a space that makes *you* want to make art, explore science, write stories, and more? If so, would you have everything you need

Blank Paper

Story Paper

Dear_____.

Letter Paper

Envelopes

Blank Cards

List Paper

Blank Books

to do what you want to do? What else could you add to enrich and deepen your child's learning experience in the play space?

Build It and They Will Come

In our home we have designated one small room as the "atelier" (an artist's studio), which is a term I learned while touring the extraordinary schools in Reggio Emilia, Italy. The ateliers in these schools are designed to give children time, information, inspiration, and materials so they can effectively express their understanding through multiple mediums. When entering the ateliers of the preschools in Reggio Emilia, I was immediately struck by the quality and beauty of both the materials and the way in which they were displayed. People often ask how the schools can use real glass vases or dishes or provide such high-quality materials to young children without having them all ruined. The beauty lies in the fact that the environment sets expectations for the children and the children rise to the occasion. If you create an environment that respects children, children learn to respect their environment.

The overall goal for an atelier is to provide interesting and engaging materials that are easily accessible and encourage meaningful, open-ended play. "If you create it, they will come." This is an important concept to consider when deciding how to use and organize your child's special spaces. With that in mind, and given the space available in your home, you can create distinct areas that invite your child to engage in the activities that represent your family's values and interests. Here are some ideas to get you started.

Writing Center

It never ceases to amaze me how a well-stocked, organized writing center can inspire spontaneous writing among young children. The goal is to create a space that invites a variety of impromptu writing by your child. By having a dedicated area stocked with writing tools, papers, and a place to work, children can independently write lists, letters, stories, or books—building writing skills through authentic and engaging writing endeavors.

We put our most commonly used materials in a utensil caddy so that it can be easily carried around the house or outside for spur-of-the-moment observational drawings or writing projects.

Recommended Materials

A variety of writing papers printed on colorful, playful paper (see "Nurturing Young Authors" in the "Printables" section on pages 199–206)

Blank note cards and envelopes

Sticky notes

Blank books (see "Book Making")

An assortment of fun pens and pencils

Fine-point permanent markers

Colored pencils

Alphabet stickers

Alphabet stamps

Interesting hole and paper punches

Tape

Glue sticks

Scissors

Erasers

A pencil sharpener

Mail Station

A great addition to any child's writing center is a family mailing station. The mailing station encourages children to take their letter writing to the next level and learn how to address and send letters to friends and loved ones. It also inspires ongoing written communication within your family.

Create mailboxes by attaching one pouch for every member of your family onto a board. It's also useful to create an address chest where you can store address labels for your closest friends and family. Ask your child whom they most often write to, and then generate a list together of people to include in your address chest. It is nice to use a multi-drawer storage container to hold the

labels (one drawer per addressee). Label each drawer with names and/or pictures. If you have space, place postage stamps in one drawer and your child's return address labels in another.

When introducing the mail station to your child, start out by writing her a letter and putting it in her pouch. Nothing stirs up more enthusiasm than receiving a personalized note right off the bat! It is also fun to take your child on a trip to the post office to hand-deliver her letters. If it is not too crowded, ask your local postal worker to explain how the letters are sent to their destinations. Some great books to inspire letter writing and mailing are *Dear Annie* by Judith Caseley, *A Letter to Amy* by Ezra Jack Keats, and *Delivering Your Mail: A Book about Mail Carriers* by Ann Owen.

Recommended Materials

Corkboard large enough to hold pouches for each member of your family

Fabric and thumbtacks for covering the corkboard (optional)

Plastic envelopes to serve as pouches (one for each member of the family, plus one extra for "outgoing mail")

Flat thumbtacks for attaching pouches to the corkboard

Labels for mail pouches, addresses, and return addresses

Storage container for storing address labels

Art Area

Art provides a wonderful outlet for young children to express their understanding of the world around them. When children have access to a variety of intriguing art materials, there is no limit to their creative endeavors.

When organizing your child's art supplies, make sure that he can access them and put them away on his own. Store materials in baskets, bins, or containers that are easy to get in and out of and that are within

your child's reach. If your child cannot easily see the material, make sure that it is labeled clearly (with a picture for nonreaders).

Some other useful tips for organizing and displaying materials are:

- Organize colored markers by color. This gives children the opportunity to appreciate all the finer nuances of color and the variations that exist within each shade.

- Place mirrors underneath supplies to display materials; this is a sure way to draw your child in for further exploration.

- Use unconventional containers for organizing materials (think outside the box). Some possibilities are pretty bowls, vases, jars,

> ### Recommended Materials
>
> A variety of wires for sculptures and models
>
> Wood scraps
>
> Fabric scraps
>
> Recycled paper scraps
>
> Thick and thin Popsicle sticks
>
> Ribbon
>
> Buttons
>
> Natural materials such as acorns, shells, seeds, pressed leaves, and flowers
>
> Fun materials such as googly eyes, sequins, and glitter
>
> Modeling clay, beeswax, and/or play dough
>
> Colored markers
>
> Crayons
>
> Oil pastels
>
> Watercolor paints
>
> Acrylic or tempera paints in red, yellow, blue, white, and black
>
> Paintbrushes in a variety of shapes and sizes
>
> Watercolor paper
>
> Drawing paper
>
> Handheld mirrors
>
> A ruler
>
> Child-size scissors

various kitchen organizers, fun hooks, or recycled bottles or cans. It adds to the fun of being in and utilizing creative spaces and materials.

I like to use high-quality art materials with young children. It introduces them to the feel and texture of materials that real artists use and allows them to bring their ideas to fruition with beautiful results. You might also keep children's books about different artists and styles of art nearby to provide ongoing inspiration.

Note: Jot down your child's thoughts during or after her process of creating; the true value of children's art can only be discovered by talking to them about their work (see "Exploration of Art and Artists"). There is *always* more to children's creations than initially meets the eye.

Science Lab

Creating an area dedicated to science and research for your children provides them the opportunity to form habits of mind that will become a natural part of how they take in new information and seek answers to their questions.

Place a basket of books with a scientific focus and some field guides near your science tools for easy access. These resources allow for easy follow-up and research on the topics that pique your child's interest.

Reading Nook

A cozy spot in the house created purely for reading sends a strong message to children about what your family values. An appealing reading nook invites children to relax and enjoy reading for pleasure's sake. Rotating the books in the reading area is a particularly effective way to maintain your child's interest and encourage regular visits.

> ### Recommended Materials
> A variety of interesting books
> A comfortable, quiet place to sit
> Good lighting for reading

Library

Involving your child in organizing your home library is an experience in and of itself. You can invite your child to sort through his books and decide what kinds of books he would like to put in baskets. Some possible categories could be: seasonal (books that rotate each season), people and feelings, poetry, alphabet and numbers, around the world, nonfiction, fairy tales, fables, and science. You could also put together easily

Recommended Materials

Picture books that relate to personal experiences

Fiction books by favorite authors

Nonfiction books on favorite topics

Books that represent different cultures, places, and traditions from around the world (see "Building a Multicultural Library" on page 151)

Several baskets or bins

Labels (with pictures for nonreaders)

accessible book baskets with other categories for different rooms in the house, such as cookbooks, art books, and building books. Involving your child in this process of building his own library gives him a new sense of ownership of his books. Not only does he know where to find the books he is looking for, he also knows where to put them when he is finished. It is helpful to clearly label each basket.

A nice variety of books in your home library will keep your child coming back for more.

Storage and Organization

When organizing your child's game, supply, or toy closet, try to keep all of his favorite things within reach in baskets or bins that are easy to take out and put away. Provide everything your child needs for an activity together within one convenient basket; for example, our "chalkboard" basket has two small chalkboards, chalk, and erasers. Attractively displaying certain items helps draw children to materials they have not used in a long time. Rotating the activities and games on your child's shelf every month or so will also encourage interaction with different activities and keep things fresh and exciting. (It is better to set aside some games and toys and just display a few activities, which will actually be used.) I am always intrigued by the way old toys take on new life when neatly organized and arranged in an appealing manner.

Over the years we have found ourselves buying fewer "toys" and more supplies and games. Supplies provide more open-ended time for explora-

tion and self-expression, while games offer a fun way for us to spend time together as a family. Toys that contain predetermined characters with preset personality traits tend to limit a child's opportunity to let their imaginations take the leading role.

Experiment with creating a few supply baskets in your Playful Learning space to encourage different learning experiences. Clearly label baskets in order to foster independent interaction with the various materials. To create easy labels, print the names of the activities, books, and materials within each basket on cover stock (heavy paper). After cutting the labels to the desired size, cover both sides with clear contact paper and then trim the edges. Punch two holes at the top of the labels, loop ribbon or twine through the holes, and tie them to the baskets with a bow. Put a dab of glue on the knot of each bow to prevent them from coming undone.

Again, try to make all necessary materials available and clearly visible to your children for any given project. Include some inspirational

Recommended Materials

Easily accessible baskets or bins

Labels (with pictures for non-readers)

Clear contact paper for covering labels

Ribbon or twine for attaching labels to baskets

art books with the art supplies to convey the message that books can be used as resources in many different ways. Our "bird watching" basket is a wonderful example of how storage and organization can encourage learning experiences. A couple of days after I put the basket together and left it out, I came downstairs after getting dressed. My oldest daughter had the whole basket in her hand and said, "Hi, Mom. We were just looking for birds. Ella saw a cardinal, and I saw a morning dove. Do you want to see our drawings?"

Displaying and Saving Children's Work

When you fashion a Playful Learning space for your children, you'll suddenly find that the work they create grows. When we make an effort to display and save our children's work in a thoughtful manner, it sends the message that their stories, art, and many creations have value. It also provides an opportunity for children to look back at their work over the years and celebrate the evolution of their learning.

There are numerous ways to artfully display your children's work. In our atelier and the girls' bedroom we have fixtures and strings that hold clips, which we use for rotating artworks that were created both at home

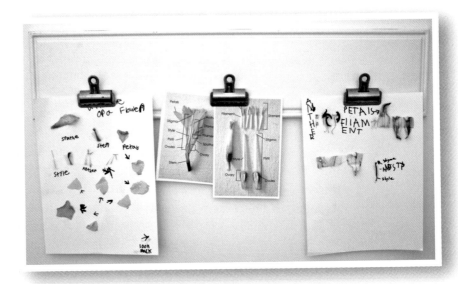

and at school. We also keep inexpensive plastic frames in various sizes handy so the girls can proudly display a special piece of work. It is nice to frame certain projects and display them in relevant areas of your home. For example, we framed the map of the girls' *from the heart* pieces and put them up near our writing center to provide ongoing writing inspiration. We framed the girls' *feeling peaceful* paintings too so they could be hung in our *place for peace*.

Along with all of the work that the girls generate at home, I am often amazed at the amount of work that comes home from school (even preschool!). After accumulating huge mounds of unsorted work, I set out to find a manageable solution.

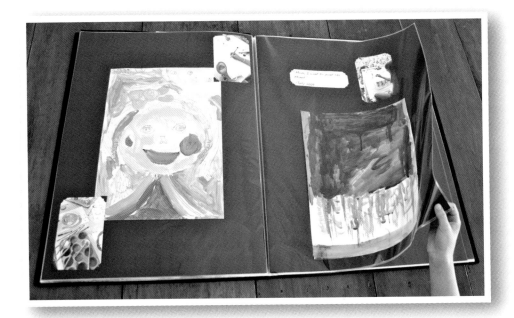

I purchased a large archival storage box (20½ × 24½ × 3 inches) for each of my children to store their work for each year. After taking the time to sort through the intimidating mound of work we had accumulated, I was pleased with the results. Now, in an effort to keep things simple, I put all of the work/art that comes home throughout the year in one large basket that I keep up high in my coat closet. It has become a tradition for all of us to sort through the work, reminisce about the fun times, and decide together which pieces we should keep at the end of each year.

In addition to keeping a box for each year, we have started portfolios for each child. The portfolios contain work and art that represent milestones in the girls' development. We have one (24 × 18 inch) portfolio for each of our daughters that currently holds their work from pre-nursery through first grade. There are plenty of pages left, which will last for years to come. The pages of the portfolios are large enough to contain artwork plus photos and quotes related to each piece. If you store a piece of work that your child created at home, it adds a wonderful dimension to include a photograph of their process or a quote they shared about their creation.

Here are a few questions to consider when deciding which work to save:

- Does it represent a leap in your child's development from one stage to another? (See the developmental overviews for each chapter.)
- Does it depict your child's interests, passions, or personality in a way that captures a certain stage, phase, or age?
- Is your child especially proud of or attached to a certain piece?
- Are you drawn to or sentimental about a particular piece of work?
- Do you have any photographs or quotes that would be fun to pull together and save to accompany a piece of work?

Recommended Materials

A variety of picture frames

Clips for hanging art

Large flat storage boxes (see the resource section)

A large portfolio (see the resource section)

A large basket for storing work as it comes home or accumulates

The effort that is required up front to create engaging spaces for your child ultimately pays off when you witness the amount of independence and self-initiation that she develops. Our atelier is the neatest room in the house because all the materials in it are clearly labeled and easily accessible. The girls are able to take out and put away everything they need on their own. With that in mind, just think about all the little changes you can make throughout your house that will significantly affect both the way your child uses the various areas in your home *and* cleans up when she is done! After reading this chapter, I invite you to take a walk around your home and note the minor adjustments that you could make that have the potential to make a major difference in the way your family interacts, connects, and grows.

PLAYFUL LEARNING EXPERIENCES

1   Nurturing Young Authors

For me, it is essential that children are deeply involved in writing, that they share with others, and that they perceive themselves as authors. I believe these three things are interconnected. A sense of authorship comes from the struggle to put something big and vital into print, and from seeing one's own printed words reach the hearts and minds of readers.

—Lucy Calkins

One of my true loves is teaching writing. What strikes me most is the transformation in attitude that takes place within a child as he discovers his true voice. When lovingly guided through the writing process, children begin to develop their inner voices and truly enjoy the effective self-expression that follows.

A well-organized writing area is an important part of supporting young authors throughout each stage of writing. As I mentioned in the "Playful Learning Spaces" section, preparing the physical environment is one of the most important aspects of facilitating successful writing activities. By making the tools for writing easily accessible and inviting, parents are sending the message to their children that writing is an important part of life.

For children to develop a productive view of themselves as authors, they must engage in meaningful writing experiences. These experiences must be relevant to their lives and allow them to successfully connect with other people. The writing activities in this chapter are meant to help young authors develop their own voice and an enthusiasm for writing. When children realize that writing is a medium for communicating their ideas and stories, the possibilities for expression become limitless.

Developmental Overview

With a little background knowledge on the stages of writing development, parents can play an important role in nurturing their young authors. Understanding how children acquire writing skills is helpful when you're trying to encourage your child's learning. Here's an overview to help you determine your child's stage in the writing process and some tips on how to help him strengthen his voice and solidify his skills.

Stage I

Drawing pictures is an important part of writing development and a powerful means of communication for young writers. Children should be encouraged to use illustrations to communicate

their ideas and stories all the way through the second grade (and even beyond). When I slow down and take the time to discuss my children's drawings with them, I am consistently impressed at the depth of thought and the amount of understanding that lie within them. What can look like simple scribbles comes alive when we listen to the stories behind them. A powerful question to ask Stage I writers is, "Can you tell me about your picture?" Asking the question in this open-ended manner allows your child to respond without any predetermined conclusions on your part. Be prepared to write your children's responses next to their drawings. When we capture their words on paper, children realize that their stories are important and that the words you write express the same message over time. Soon they will begin to "write" stories themselves beside their pictures. The scribbles you see by their pictures and on the note cards and writing paper left out in their writing area are a wonderful sign that your young writer has learned that writing communicates his ideas to the world.

Stage II

As children learn about the alphabet and start to recognize letters in the world around them, they enjoy incorporating them into their writing. When letters first make an appearance in Stage II writing, they seem to have no rhyme or reason. The letters that appear in this stage are simply the ones a child has learned to recognize and copy. It may be the letters in your child's name or merely letters that happen to be visible to them at the time they are writing. Once a child is comfortable writing a letter, you will see it appear often in his or her work. It is important to continue to take dictation from writers during Stage II,

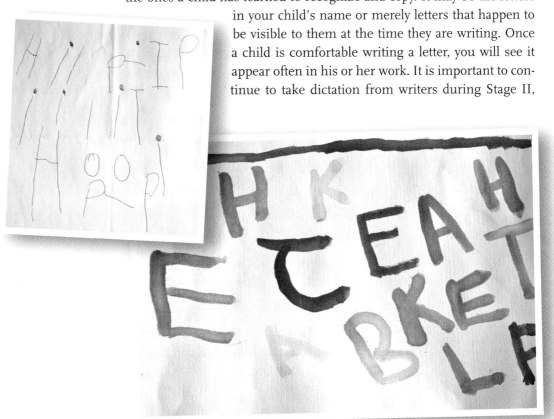

recording their comments about what they are writing. Although you might find their writing undecipherable, it may contain powerful messages. During Stage II it is important to have a tabletop alphabet chart (see "Alphabet Chart" in "Printables" on page 197) clearly visible in your child's writing area.

Stage III

In Stage III writing, children become fascinated with writing "readable" words. They start asking parents and teachers about the correct way to spell the words they want to write. The goal for children during this stage of writing is to recognize and write one to two sounds per word. As parents we can help our children by drawing their attention to the sounds they hear in the word that they want to spell. Be sure to pronounce the word slowly, emphasizing each individual sound. Some good questions to ask your child are, "What is the first sound you hear in the word h- h-hat?" Then you can ask, "What is the next sound you hear in the word h- a- a- at?" If your child can't identify the correct letter for the sound, simply tell her the letter. Having an alphabet chart (see "Alphabet Chart" in "Printables" on page 197) handy in your writing area can also aid this process.

During Stage III writing, it is more valuable for a child to correctly identify one or two sounds independently than to correctly spell a word with the assistance of an adult. Once a child knows how to slowly pronounce the words that she wants to spell, she has the foundation to write on her own. Now, I am the first to admit that this process can be painstaking at times. I will also confess that there are moments when it is easier for me to tell my children all of the letters in a word they want to spell than to wait for them to discover the sounds themselves. Yet in the long run, taking the time to help them identify the sounds and thus discern the letters, the *majority* of the time, results in confident and independent writers.

My oldest daughter is a perfectionist, and even after successfully identifying a few sounds in a word she was writing, she often wanted to know if it was spelled the "real" way. I used these moments to explain to her that when children are learning to write, they don't need to spell every word correctly; they just need to write down as many sounds as they can hear and identify. I would go on to explain that young writers are thinking about so many things (what they want to say, how to write letters, how to spell words) that the most important thing for them to do is get their ideas down on the paper. It took a few of these conversations for my daughter to internalize my message, yet once she did her writing really freed up. She was less inhibited and started writing independently for longer periods of time.

You will also notice that during this stage of writing children often forget to put spaces between their words. The lack of spaces combined with a child using only one or two letters per word can make reading your child's work back to them a bit challenging. This can be lovingly addressed by explaining to them that spaces between words help readers to understand someone's writing. A good strategy is to show them how to use their finger to create the necessary space. Once they write a word, they can put their finger on the paper and start the next word on the other side of their finger. You could jokingly read a book as if there were no spaces between the words and point out how funny it would sound and how hard it would be to understand books if the author did not remember to put spaces between his words.

The strong link between reading and writing development becomes evident during Stage III writing. The alphabet activities presented in "The Joy of Reading" will help children strengthen their letter-sound recognition. The more readily children can correlate a sound with the corresponding letter, the smoother the writing experience will be for her. With that being said, it is important that the process of learning letters and their sounds be joyful and lighthearted.

Stage IV

Children who begin to use writing to communicate more complex stories and ideas have entered Stage IV. Stage IV writers are developing a stronger personal voice and can work independently for longer periods of time. They still rely heavily on listening to sounds in words, but they are building a repertoire of basic words that they know how to read and write from memory. A rich and engaging writing area in the home can be a haven for Stage IV writers, a place where they can spend time of their own accord. I can't seem to keep our writing area stocked with enough blank books for our oldest daughter. She is happily developing a library of her own stories that she and her sister love to read over and over.

Facilitating the phonetic spelling discussed in Stage III is still an important role for parents of children in Stage IV of their writing development. One question that often comes from parents of Stage IV writers

is, "How will my child ever learn to spell words correctly if I am encouraging him to just listen for a few sounds?" In the beginning of Stage III and throughout Stage IV, it can feel like a leap of faith to *not* encourage correct spelling in your child's writing. Yet by focusing on the independent recognition of sounds rather than simply copying down letters, your child is developing a deep understanding of phonetics and the important habit of analyzing words. As an adult, when I ask for the spelling of a word from a colleague, I will write the response without actually being conscious of the letters I am being told. Children do the same thing when we give them the correct spelling of a word: they may get the word right in the moment, yet retain nothing from the experience. Over time, as children become more facile with the phonetic code, you will see that knowledge transfer to their writing. It does happen, and it is an extraordinary process to witness!

Not only does correct spelling begin to take shape in Stage IV writing, punctuation and grammar do too. Once a child reaches Stage IV, you will see that he slowly starts to incorporate all the lessons he is learning in school. For instance, in first grade when periods are introduced, you will see a multitude of periods throughout your child's writing. This plethora of periods, although they are not necessarily properly placed, represents a healthy experimentation by your child. And just as with spelling, experimentation with punctuation will lead to its correct use. Experimentation with and incorporation of newly acquired skills continue throughout the early elementary years, until, as he grows older, your child's writing becomes more conventional and consistent.

The learning experiences in this chapter have been specifically chosen to provide children with authentic ways to express themselves through writing. Young writers in all stages of development can successfully complete these activities. Keep your child's stage in mind, and provide any necessary support to ensure that your child has a successful experience. Never hesitate to take dictation or encourage your child to illustrate her ideas; the goal is to create meaningful shared experiences with your child and your family.

MAKING LISTS

List making is a great place for budding young writers to start their careers. Even the youngest children can feel successful as they learn to write down the sounds they hear for each word on their list. Writing lists offers your child the opportunity to experience writing in an authentic, real-world context, whether it is documenting what he wants from the grocery store or what he will pack for a trip. Encouraging list making is also a great way to teach your child the value of planning ahead.

ONE STEP AHEAD

Children love to mimic what they see the grown-ups in their lives doing. Become a list-making model; talk to your child about the types of lists you create and show him how you use lists in your everyday life. You will be amazed at the lists you see popping up around the house!

Materials

List Paper printable, printed on a variety of fun papers (see page 198)

Pens and pencils

Alphabet Chart printable (see page 197)

THE PROCESS

Reading one of the picture books from the following list is a great way to have your child begin his list-making adventures. If these books aren't available to you, start by modeling and explaining list making.

Invite your child to create a list that is relevant to a current interest or event. Some possible list-making topics could be: ingredients for a recipe, things to do during vacations or breaks from school, items to pack for a trip, plans for birthday parties, or groceries to buy.

Be sure to keep list paper out for your children to spontaneously grab when the need for a list comes to mind.

> **Books to Inspire**
>
> *Oliver's Must-Do List* by Susan Taylor Brown
>
> *Wallace's Lists* by Barbara Bottner and Gerald Kruglik

MORE TO EXPLORE

Encourage your child to try his hand at writing list poems. Choose an object that inspires him (such as a tree, an insect, a flower, or a favorite toy), and invite him to write a list of words that describe that item. He will be proud of how poetic his descriptive words sound when read together.

BEST PART OF ME

My Hands
I like holding stuff with them
I love to move them
I like to pick up stuff with them
I like to talk with them
I like to play with them

Inviting your child to learn from and incorporate writing strategies used by other writers into her own work offers unlimited inspiration and encourages your child to see herself as a true author. *The Best Part of Me* by Wendy Ewald provides a great opportunity for children to relate to the words of other children and to see how they can weave photography into their writing experience. This activity is also great for developing a healthy self-image as well as a good catalyst for discussions about how we are all different and the same.

For this experience I recommend reading *The Best Part of Me* for inspiration and then using a camera to capture your child's "best part," but this activity could easily be achieved by initiating a conversation with your child about the best part of her and then inviting her to draw the part of herself that she appreciates the most.

> **Materials**
>
> A camera
>
> Writing supplies
>
> Alphabet Chart printable (see page 197)

ONE STEP AHEAD

Before engaging in this experience with your child, give some thought to what you think is the best part of yourself. Think of an imaginative way to sketch or photograph your best asset and then participate in the activity with your child. Try thinking beyond just body parts. Maybe the best part of yourself is your imagination; how could you represent that?

THE PROCESS

It is a good idea to start learning experiences by posing a question or making a statement that piques your child's curiosity and grabs her attention. For this activity, I started out by telling my girls that I had an important question for them. When they asked me what it was, I told them that I needed to read them a special book before I could ask them. Well, at this point they were so curious that they begged me to read them the book.

When your child is interested, read *The Best Part of Me* to them. The book consists of photographs and writing by children. Each child featured in the book was asked to choose and write about the best part of himself or herself. The text is actually printed in the child's own handwriting, which creates a real connection between the authors and the reader.

> **Books to Inspire**
>
> *The Best Part of Me: Children Talk about Their Bodies in Pictures and Words* by Wendy Ewald
>
> *Secret Games: Collaborative Works with Children 1969–1999* by Wendy Ewald

When you've finished the book, ask your child, "What is the best part of you?" Keep a camera or drawing supplies close at hand, so your child can promptly begin planning how to illustrate her best parts.

Later, invite your child to write or dictate some words to go with the photos or drawings she made. A nice idea is to place the photos or drawings on the same paper as the words and then proudly display them in your home.

MORE TO EXPLORE

Expand the concept of "the best part of . . ." to encompass your family, school, or community. Invite your child to consider ways in which she can capture her ideas through photos, drawings, and words. What is the best part of your family?

FROM THE HEART

By creating a map of their heart, children bring to the forefront the things that matter most to them. The memories, passions, people, and places a child cares most deeply about make the best topics for writing about. This experience comes from Georgia Heard's book *Awakening the Heart* and can be used as a precursor to keeping a notebook, to help generate ideas for writing stories. Keep the completed piece near your child's writing center for ongoing inspiration.

Materials

Watercolor paper

Fine-point permanent markers

Watercolor paints

Alphabet Chart printable (see page 197)

ONE STEP AHEAD

Have some suggestions in mind for your child so you can offer him ideas if he gets stuck. Some things to consider are: favorite people, places, hobbies, sports, music, food, memories, books, and areas of study. Be prepared to generate a map of your own heart. It will inspire your child, and open up a new avenue for connecting and sharing with each other.

THE PROCESS

A fun way to introduce this experience is by reading *My Map Book* by Sara Fanelli. *My Map Book* is a wonderful picture book that walks the reader through a variety of vividly illustrated maps of a child's bedroom, neighborhood, tummy, heart, and so on.

After reading the book start a discussion with your child about the fact that authors write about things they love and hold close to their hearts. You could pose the question, "If you drew a map of your heart, what would you include?" If your child has a hard time thinking of ideas, you may want to share what you would add to a map of your heart.

Give your child a piece of watercolor paper with an outline of a large heart. Encourage him to start filling in the heart with all of the things he loves. (We used thin Sharpie markers, so the ink did not bleed when the girls painted over their drawings.) My oldest daughter used phonetic spelling to write all of the words in her heart. My youngest drew pictures and then dictated the words she wanted me to write down on her heart. When your child is finished, invite him to fill in his heart with watercolor paints.

Books to Inspire

My Map Book by Sara Fanelli

MORE TO EXPLORE

Invite your child to create other maps such as: a map of his family, a map of his room, or a map of his face. Encourage your child to write labels identifying the different parts of his maps. It is wonderful to do this activity year after year and see how it evolves for your child over time.

WRITING STORIES

Children have so many stories to tell. Writing their stories down and sharing them with others allows children to communicate ideas and share their thoughts with other people. Collecting your child's stories over time and revisiting them every now and again is a wonderful way to celebrate her growth.

Our youngest daughter writes a how-to book on making play dough figures.

Materials

Story Paper printables 1–5, depending on your child's writing stage (see pages 199–203)

Blank books (see pages 50–54)

Pens and pencils

Colored pencils for illustrations

Alphabet Chart printable (see page 197)

ONE STEP AHEAD

The desire to write stories and make books comes naturally to young children. Simply prepare an inviting space for writing with interesting writing papers and utensils, and you will be impressed by the amount of story writing you see taking place. Include a variety of story papers and blank books with your child's writing materials.

THE PROCESS

It is helpful to encourage children to write stories from their lives. While I never dissuade my children from writing a fictional story that they are excited about, I have found that when young children write about the meaningful events, people, and places in their lives, their writing has more depth and personal relevance. By learning to bring their memories, passions, and thoughts to life, children can more readily find their true voice. Listen closely to the stories that your child tells throughout the day and let him know when one is worthy of writing down and would make a good book.

Children's illustrations are an important part of their storytelling process. Young children often enjoy illustrating their stories first and then writing their stories or dictating them to you. Lots of blank lines can be intimidating to emerging writers. Select the story paper that best suits your child's writing abilities. As he progresses, introduce story paper with more lines.

> **Books to Inspire**
>
> *The Best Story* by Eileen Spinelli
>
> *A Book* by Mordicai Gerstein

If your child gets stuck or is at a loss for what to write, offer suggestions from stories that he has told you or from shared memories. Celebrate your child's success by sharing his stories with friends and loved ones. Let your child know how powerful his words are and that when he writes down his ideas, thoughts, and stories, many people can enjoy them.

MORE TO EXPLORE

Create a basket in your home library that is exclusively for books written by your child. Revisit his stories often and treat them as valued books in your collection.

KEEPING A NOTEBOOK

Keeping a writer's notebook is a key element to what Lucy Calkins would refer to as "living the writerly life."[1] It encourages children to live life like true writers do—capturing the small details of daily life in order to turn them into big stories. Collecting thoughts, questions, memories, quotes, and so on in one place creates a treasure chest of inspiration for your child's writing—the ultimate solution to the "I don't know what to write about" conundrum.

> **Materials**
>
> A special notebook hand-selected by your child
>
> Fun pens and pencils
>
> Time to wonder, observe, listen, think, question, and dream
>
> Alphabet Chart printable (see page 197)

ONE STEP AHEAD

Keep a writer's notebook of your own. It is a wonderful reminder to slow down and capture the magical things in our lives. It is easier to introduce your child to the concept of keeping a notebook if you have already started one—even if you have only jotted down a couple of thoughts. Sharing your entries with your children also brings you closer as a family and can create a tradition that will be enjoyed for years (maybe even generations) to come.

THE PROCESS

If you have started a writer's notebook of your own, share your notebook with your child. It is especially fun if you have written about a memory that involves your child; it will help him connect to the experience. Explain that you use your notebook to collect your thoughts, ideas, drawings, questions, lists, memories, and so on.

Invite your child to select or make a notebook that he would really love to write in. It is important that your child feel a personal connection to his notebook. Encourage him to make it his own by adding decorations, drawings, or pictures from magazines. For very young writers, I would recommend blank pages so they can focus on drawing without getting overwhelmed by all the blank lines.

Explain to your child that his notebook is a special place just for him. He can write lots of words or no words. He can draw pictures, write poems, add lists—use it for capturing whatever he wants. Be sure he understands that he doesn't have to worry about his letters looking perfect or spelling words correctly (that comes later); it is simply a place for him to get down his ideas.

Keep your child's notebook and favorite pen or pencil handy at all times. My daughters like to keep them right next to their beds and often ask if they can write before falling asleep.

MORE TO EXPLORE

Once your child has done a lot of writing in his notebook, invite him to select one of his favorite entries to develop a bit further. A couple of options might be for him to write a poem on a nice piece of paper and paint a picture to complement it, or to select a favorite memory to expand upon and make into a book.

> **Books to Inspire**
>
> *Amelia's Notebook* by Marissa Moss (for older writers)
>
> *Ish* by Peter H. Reynolds
>
> *Wilfrid Gordon MacDonald Partridge* by Mem Fox

LETTER WRITING

Writing letters is an authentic way for children to learn that writing is used to communicate and connect with other people. When your child engages in the letter-writing process, she practices proper letter forma-

> **Materials**
>
> Letter Paper printables 1–3, depend-
> ing on the stage of your child (see
> pages 204–206)
>
> Blank note cards
>
> Alphabet stickers and stamps
>
> Pens and pencils
>
> Colored pencils
>
> Alphabet Chart Printable (see page
> 197)

tion and solidifies her ability to connect the correct sound to each letter. To add to your child's letter writing experience, set up her very own mail station (see page 18).

ONE STEP AHEAD

Keep your child's writing center stocked with fun letter papers, blank cards, and envelopes. It is exciting to witness the independent letter writing that follows.

THE PROCESS

A great way to create excitement about letter writing is by reading *The Jolly Postman or Other People's Letters* by Allan and Janet Ahlberg. The book consist of letters written to famous fairy-tale characters and is written in an engaging format where children get to open the envelopes and see the letters firsthand.

Once the excitement about letter writing is sparked, it simply becomes a matter of keeping your child's writing area stocked with interesting paper, note cards, and envelopes. With all emergent writers, drawing pictures is an important way of communicating meaning. It is for this reason that three types of Letter Paper printables are provided in the back of the book: Letter Paper 1 allows beginning writers to focus on drawing images, Letter Paper 2 provides a space for drawing and writing, while Letter Paper 3 contains only lines. Try to print the appropriate Letter Paper for your child on a variety of interesting papers. Who can resist a fresh and lovely assortment of stationery?

It can also be fun to print out return address labels with your child's name. The personalized labels give your child an opportunity to learn about addressing and mailing her letters.

> **Books to Inspire**
>
> *Dear Mr. Blueberry* by Simon James
>
> *Dear Tooth Fairy* by Alan Durant
>
> *The Jolly Postman or Other People's Letters* by Allan and Janet Ahlberg
>
> *Toot and Puddle* by Holly Hobbie

MORE TO EXPLORE

Once your child becomes comfortable writing basic letters, you can expand her experience by encouraging her to create handmade birthday cards, invitations, Valentine's Day cards, and thank-you letters.

BOOK MAKING

Basic blank books are a must-have for any house with young, budding authors. Simply having the books around inspires spontaneous story writing. Younger children can participate by selecting the colors of the covers, paper, binding, and so on. Older children can begin making simple books on their own. Below are three different tutorials for easy-to-make blank books.

ONE STEP AHEAD

I can't emphasize enough the benefits of having premade blank books available in your child's writing center. I usually make six to ten at a time and am always surprised at how quickly they are utilized. It is a joy to see wonderful stories, how-to books, and journals pop up around the house!

TWIG BOOKS

Twig books can be used for many different types of handmade books. They are especially well suited for nature journals, field guides, and memory books.

Materials

One to two 8 ½ x 11 inch sheets of cover stock paper

Two to six sheets of 8 ½ x 11 inch blank white paper or Story Paper printables 1–5, depending on your child's writing stage (see pages 199–203)

A hole punch

One twig, about ¼ inch in diameter and the height of your book

One large, thick rubber band

THE PROCESS

First decide what size book you would like to make. Books can be made with whole 8½ x 11 inch pages or by folding the pages in half. It is fun to make books of different shapes and sizes. With the cover stock paper as the front and back page and approximately four to six pieces of paper in between, align the pages and then punch two holes on the left-hand side of the paper: one inch from the top and one inch from the bottom.

Select a twig that's the height of the book or slightly smaller. Line up the twig with the holes, wrap the rubber band around the top of twig, and then string it through the top hole. Stretch the rubber band down the back of the book. Then string it through the bottom hole, toward the front of the book, and around the bottom of the twig. Open the book and crease the front cover along the twig for easy access.

CLOTHBOUND BOOKS

Clothbound books are great multipurpose books that will hold up well after repeated readings. They are a wonderful choice for stocking your child's writing center to encourage story writing.

Materials

One to two sheets of 8½ x 11 inch cover stock paper

Two to six sheets of 8½ x 11 inch blank white or Story Paper printables 1–5, depending on your child's writing stage (see pages 199–203)

A stapler and staples

Cloth tape, two inches wide by the height of your book

THE PROCESS

First decide what size book you would like to make. Books can be made with whole 8½ x 11 inch pages or by folding the pages in half. With the cover stock as the front and back page and approximately four to six pieces of paper in between, staple the pages together approximately one-fourth inch in from one of the sides. Cut a piece of cloth tape to match the height of the book and apply it along the spine of the book, covering the staples.

RING BOOKS

Ring books are a good choice for young children who would like to be involved in making their own books. Even the smallest hands can help to successfully assemble these easy-to-make books.

Materials

One to two sheets of 8 ½ x 11 inch cover stock paper

Two to six sheets of 8 ½ x 11 inch blank white or Story Paper printables 1–5,

depending on your child's writing stage (see pages 199–203)

A hole punch

Two loose-leaf book rings (we used one-inch rings, but you could go smaller)

THE PROCESS

First decide what size book you would like to make. Books can be made with whole 8 ½ x 11 inch pages or by folding the pages in half. With the cover stock as the front and back pages and approximately four to six pieces of paper in between, punch two holes on the left-hand side of the paper approximately one inch from the top and one inch from the bottom. Simply secure all the pages by placing the rings through the holes.

Web Sites to Inspire

Bookmaking with Kids, www.bookmakingwithkids.com

Susan Kapuscinski Gaylord's Making Books with Children, www.making books.com

MORE TO EXPLORE

If a piece of writing takes on a lot of momentum or personal significance for your child, you can help her bind it. It might be a piece that she has written at school or something written on Story Paper (see "Story Paper" in "Printables") at home. Taking the time to create a book for a special piece of writing together with your child shows her that you value her work and that her words have had a positive impact on you. Again, it is fun to add her "published" books to the book basket you have set aside specifically for her writing.

2   The Joy of Reading

It is not enough to simply teach children to read; we have to give them something worth reading. Something that will stretch their imaginations—something that will help them make sense of their own lives and encourage them to reach out toward people whose lives are quite different from their own.

— Katherine Paterson

Being in the presence of a child who is learning to read is a magical experience. Throughout my time in classrooms and in observing my own two children, I have realized that the process is unique for every child. The building blocks or necessary skills are the same, but how they come together for each child is as distinctive as the child himself.

When parents are aware of the essentials that form the foundation of good reading, you can actively participate and share in your child's development. This chapter provides you with insight into your child's reading development so you will know what to watch for and how to support your child's reading experiences. Following is an overview on how reading skills develop over time in children ages three to eight.

Developmental Overview

Stage I

Parents can really help set the stage for their children to enjoy a lifetime of reading. The first and most important step is to read together and read together often, so even the youngest children begin to associate positive feelings with reading.[1] With the tiniest readers, spending one-on-one time reading together and developing a love for your family's favorite stories is the most valuable thing you can do. You will find that your young reader will grow fond of certain stories and ask you to read them over and over again. Reading favorite stories a number of times is beneficial to your child on many levels. It helps her learn that words have meanings, which remain consistent and are the same every time they are read. Your child also takes in the nuances of tone and inflection that are present when you read with expression. It will be fun to observe your child as she begins to use the same intonations that you use when she moves into Stage II and begins to "read" books from memory.

As you read, it is helpful to move your finger along the text. Pointing to each word as you go subtly relays the message to your child that each word is distinct and holds its own meaning. Eventually your child will develop the same habit, which will serve her well as her own reading takes off.

Another enjoyable activity is discussing the illustrations within the book you are reading together. After reading the text, ask your child if she can identify different aspects of what you just read in the pictures, such as the characters, actions, or setting. Looking at pictures for clues is a strategy that all young readers should utilize when beginning to read independently. The more they explore the connections between illustrations and text with you, the sooner it will become natural to them.

Stage I readers delight in books with simple text that often repeats itself. They love the predictability and will often chime in to help complete your sentences. Choosing books that have illustrations that accurately depict the story is not only enjoyable for the youngest readers, but will also come in handy as your child begins to read on her own. Alphabet, counting, and songbooks are all great for Stage I readers.

Stage II

A wonderful milestone that occurs in Stage II is when your child begins memorizing and reciting his favorite stories. While teaching, I often heard parents express concern over the fact that their child had memorized his book rather than actually reading it. Please allow me to put that concern to rest—the skill of reading books from memory is actually an important achievement in a child's development. When a child "reads" these favorite stories, while running his fingers over the words, he is building essential skills that will soon help him recognize individual letter sounds and words. If you give your child the freedom to recite books to you, it won't be long before he is actually recognizing and sounding out the words that lie before him.

Stage II is a good time to start nurturing the recognition of letters and their sounds (playfully) with your child through reading, simple games, and activities. As your child's knowledge of letters and their sounds grows, he will begin to recognize them in his favorite stories, which marks the beginning of his independent reading.

When you notice your child making the transition from memorizing to recognizing words, there are fun and easy things you can do while reading with your child to help him expand his newfound skills. Consider the following:

- As you read aloud to your child, pause when you get to the last word of a sentence and let your child fill in the blank.

- Before you read a story, place sticky notes over a couple of words, showing just the first letter. When you come upon the words, ask your child to predict what each word says. This encourages your child to recognize words based on their first letter, as well as to gather what a word might be from the context of the story.

- After finishing a story, invite your child to flip back through the book and find all of the words that start with *B*s, *M*s, and so on.

- Continue to encourage your child to move a finger across the words while reading. Once your child begins to recognize words within the text, have him go even slower and touch each word as he reads.

Getting your child a library card of her own and making frequent trips there together to find new and exciting books go a long way in nurturing a love of books within your child. During our library visits I spend some time with each of my daughters, helping them find a couple of books that fit their individual reading level. I also give them time to peruse the books independently so they can make their own selections based on current interests.

I must admit that until recently I was a children's literature snob. Having been immersed and well versed in the classics, I wanted to expose my children to only the best. What I learned really quickly, however, as I tried to censor the choices the girls were making, was that I was actually subtly (or not so subtly) discouraging them from choosing books for pure pleasure. Once this lightbulb went on for me and I let my daughters have free choice (as long as the books were age and content appropriate) of their reading material, their love of reading soared. One way to still sneak in your favorite titles is to suggest that your child choose one book for bedtime reading and you choose one too. Another way to slip in essential reading is to take solo trips to the library every so often and simply leave your selections out at home on a coffee table or by their bed; it won't be long before your child climbs into your lap and asks you to read your selection to her.

Stage III

Stage III is that magical time when you begin to see all the little pieces come together—the vocabulary your child has developed from being read and spoken to combines with a recognition of letters and a knowledge of their sounds. My youngest daughter is currently in Stage III, and I will never forget the night that she picked up a book she had never read before and tirelessly read every single word. As she pointed to each word and sounded it out, I realized how important it was for her to have a rich vocabulary, which primarily comes from reading aloud together for many years. She was able to read words because they were familiar to her; she had seen them many times in different contexts, and when she needed that personal connection in order to read certain words, it was there for her. My daughter's ability to recognize letters and her knowledge of their sounds along with the habit she had developed of noticing and pointing to every word on the page came together for her that night as she read her first book from cover to cover.

As I mentioned earlier, the learning process is different for every child. This alchemy that I witnessed happens at different ages for different children, just as children learn to walk at different times in their lives. Children lean on various strategies to get them through the beginning stages of reading, so the synthesis is distinct for each individual. The important thing to keep in mind is the attitude that is developing along with the skills; although the skills are essential, your child's mind-set is what determines whether he will maintain what we as parents all hope for—a lifelong love of reading.

Selecting books that are a good match for your child (see "Choosing the Right Books" next) is essential for Stage III readers. Newly emergent readers walk a fine line between euphoria and disenchantment when it comes to their attitude toward reading. It is essential that they experience success, which means that they need access to books that fit their ability. There is no rush to have your child reading more advanced books; there is plenty of time for that. Enjoy this stage and spend as long as your child needs reading her favorites over and over again, celebrating her accomplishment each time. Now is a good time to take out her favorite board books that you read to her when she was younger. Encourage her to point to each word as she reads along. After a while, your child will realize that she can actually read each word rather than just recite it from memory.

If your child wants to take on books that she has not read before, suggest to her that you take turns; you read the story to her first and then she can read it to you. Having your child hear the story first can go a long way in helping her successfully read it back to you. Some of the strategies that you can encourage your child to use when trying to read words on her own are to: look at the first letter of a word, look at pictures for clues, and keep reading to see if it makes sense.

Stage IV

As children begin to master basic decoding of the English language, they move into a different level of reading and need to focus on developing new skills. I have heard it said well: children evolve from *learning to read* into *reading to learn*. In this stage readers focus on developing strategies for comprehension. You can help your child during this stage of development by encouraging him to make connections between the books he is reading and himself, other books, and the world.[2]

Stage IV readers also make great researchers and love looking up interesting facts and trivia independently. Up until this point your child has probably experienced nonfiction texts as read-alouds or has curiously flipped the pages, looking at the photos or illustrations. Now you can surround your child with a variety of nonfiction books that are in line with his current reading level and contain topics of interest. Simple how-to books are especially empowering for a child in Stage IV, as he can use his reading skills to accomplish new and exciting things, such as making paper airplanes, sewing simple projects, exploring the art of origami, or even trying out new hairstyles. Now is the time to capitalize on your child's enthusiasm for any given topic and explore, extend, and enrich it through books.

Choosing the Right Books

When children begin reading on their own, it is critical that they read books that are at the correct reading level. Children become better readers by reading books fluently and often. Too many bumps in the road (such as unknown words) can stifle enthusiasm and comprehension. When your child reads books that match his reading ability, he will experience the joy that comes from reading with ease, understanding the story, and experiencing success from cover to cover—quite an accomplishment!

Nothing encourages a child to pick up a book and read it more than when he has access to books he feels successful reading. It is really worth the time to go to a library or bookstore and preselect books that are a good fit for your child. Of course your solo trips will not replace visits to libraries and bookstores with your children. They are simply an opportunity for you to have the right books at your fingertips when your child shows an interest in reading.

One way to know whether the book your child is reading is a proper match for him is to keep in mind that your child should be able to independently read approximately 95 percent of the words on the page without any difficulty. If he is stumbling on more than 5 percent of the words, the book is too difficult.

However, if your child is just starting to read, the 95 percent guideline is not much help. For me, the most difficult time to find books that suited my daughters was when they where just entering Stage III of their reading development. This is the stage when they are ready to start reading alone but can become disengaged quickly if what they are reading is too difficult. The most important things to look for when selecting a book for this stage are:

- Text that accurately coincides with the illustrations
- Text that contains simple words that are a part of your child's everyday vocabulary
- Text that is repetitive and predictable
- Pages with no more than one or two sentences each

Some of our favorite early readers for children on the cusp of cracking the phonetic code are:

Brown Bear, Brown Bear, What Do You See? by Bill Martin Jr.

The Chick and the Duckling by Mirra Ginsburg

Have You Seen My Cat? by Eric Carle

Have You Seen My Duckling? By Nancy Tafuri

I Went Walking by Sue Williams

If at First… by Sandra Boynton

Let's Play by Leo Lionni

Mrs. Wishy-Washy Makes a Splash! by Joy Cowley

Once your child is reading these initial books fluently, you can more easily rely on the 95 percent accuracy rule of thumb to determine whether a book is a good match for him (after time, your child should be able to determine this on his own). It is also important to note here that it is all right for your child to occasionally read books that are too easy or a bit challenging for him. When a child is attracted or excited about a book that is *not* a good fit, my advice is to let him run with it. It is just as important to nurture a child's love of books as it is to develop his skills.

When reading with your child, be sure to introduce him to the importance of reading books that are a good fit for him. You could start out by telling him that the best way for children to become better readers is to read books that are "just right" for them. Explain that if he is always reading books that are too hard, he may not understand the story (this is especially important for younger siblings who want to read what their older brother or sister is reading). Next discuss the fact that if he is always reading books that are too easy, he will not grow to be a better reader. Go on to explain that a book that is a good fit is one where he can read almost every word on every page.

To encourage reading, select a basket or bin together in which you will store your child's "just right" books. Invite your child to select a few books that feel like a good fit to put into his basket or bin (if your child is not reading independently yet and is reciting books from memory, that is okay). Add some of your child's favorite books (especially books that you have been reading together for many years). Invite your child to make a label for the basket so he begins to feel a sense of ownership of the basket and the books that go into it.

Keep your child's just-right book basket near his bed, and invite him to read to you during your bedtime routine. We enjoy reading one book to our daughters and then having them read one book to us each night. Check in with your child about the books in his just-right basket from time to time. Children love to feel that they have mastered certain books and enjoy the process of selecting new ones to explore.

Along with understanding how your child's reading abilities develop and helping him to choose the right books, there are many fun and engaging ways to nurture his appreciation of letters, sounds, words, and stories. The following experiences will help you guide your child through all of his stages of development and will nurture a fascination and appreciation for both the written and spoken word.

ALPHABET PHOTOGRAPHY

Alphabet books are a wonderful addition to your home library. Collecting, comparing, and contrasting the many interesting varieties is a wonderful way to share time together. But alas, no alphabet book collection is complete without a homemade version to call your own.

When your child creates her own alphabet book, she will really take ownership of the content, thus processing the letters, sounds, and words on a deeper level. This learning experience helps children recognize the letters of the alphabet and learn the sounds associated with each letter. After doing this activity with my own girls, I was able to refer back to the words they had selected for each letter as prompts to help them remember each letter's sound.

ONE STEP AHEAD

This experience takes a while, so don't hesitate to spread it out over a couple of days. Gather some of your child's favorite alphabet books and look through them together to inspire some ideas.

Materials

A camera

Photo paper

A blank book (see pages 50–54)

Glue stick

THE PROCESS

After reading some of your favorite alphabet books together, mention the possibility of creating your child's very own alphabet book. Explain that she could make her own alphabet book by taking pictures of things that represent each letter of the alphabet. One example you could mention is taking a picture of her to represent the first letter in her name.

Before you pull out the camera, start coming up with ideas for each letter. It is helpful to consult your own ABC book collection (or visit a local library) to start formulating ideas. When your child is ready, help her set up and photograph each item. As I mentioned earlier, thinking of and setting up a photo for twenty-six different letters takes a long time. You may want to spread it our over multiple days. Also, while it is wonderful to have your child take all the photographs, you may want to take a backup shot of each picture just in case some don't turn out.

Once all the photographs are taken, decide how you will add text to your photos. If you are using a photography program on your computer, you can add the text directly to the photograph.

After all the photos have been printed, invite your child to help you lay them out in alphabetical order. Mount the photos in a blank book and, if you didn't add words directly onto the photo, write the text underneath each picture on the book page. Add your finished book to your alphabet book collection and return to it occasionally for inspiration.

> ### Books to Inspire
>
> *Alphabatics* by Suse MacDonald
>
> *Alphabeasties and Other Amazing Types* by Sharon Werner and Sarah Forss
>
> *Bruno Munari's ABC* by Bruno Munari
>
> *Charley Harper ABC's* by Charley Harper
>
> *A Child's Day: An Alphabet of Play* by Ida Pearle
>
> *Museum ABC* by the Metropolitan Museum of Art

MORE TO EXPLORE

Create a basket that houses all of the books that your child "publishes." If your alphabet book is the first entry, create more together; some possibilities are counting books, cookbooks, and stories that your child writes.

It is also fun to create an alphabet book by walking through town together and taking photos of each letter as your child finds them on signs, in menus, or on whatever is around you. Try discovering the letters within nature patterns too.

ALPHABET SEARCH

Engaging in an alphabet search is a great way for your child to strengthen her letter recognition and familiarity with the sounds of each letter. What I love about this activity is that while it helps with letter identification, the emphasis is on solidifying the sounds of letters. When my youngest daughter drew the *B* card, she ran around the house saying the sound over and over again until she found an object that matched the same sound.

Materials

Alphabet Cards printable
    (see page 207)
Card stock (optional)
Everyday household items

ONE STEP AHEAD

Prepare for this experience by printing and cutting out the Alphabet Cards printable. I glued mine to card stock for added durability. It also helps to have some household items in mind that start with the letters that are more difficult to pair with objects, such as *w, x,* and *z.* Some examples might be *window* for *w, xylophone* for *x,* and *zipper* for *z.*

To play, shuffle the alphabet cards and place them in a pile. Invite your child to select a card and then find an item in the house that starts with the same sound as the letter they chose. If just you and your child are playing this game together, each of you can go find an item and then meet back at the "base" to share what you discovered.

Repeat until all of the letters have been selected.

If you are playing this game with more than one child and they are at different levels of understanding, you can challenge the older one by telling him to find an item that contains the letter rather than an item that starts with the letter.

Books to Inspire

ABC Kids by Laura Ellen Williams

Alphabet Explosion: Search and Count from Alien to Zebra by John Nickle

Eating the Alphabet: Fruits and Vegetables from A to Z by Lois Ehlert

---

MORE TO EXPLORE

As your child becomes well versed in the letters and sounds of the alphabet, you can add letter combinations, such as sh, ch, and ph.

BUILDING WORDS

Building words is a wonderful activity for children who are on the verge of reading. This learning experience will encourage your child to isolate and learn each distinct sound within words and also helps her learn how to blend individual sounds together to form a word.

> **Materials**
>
> Build-a-Word Set printables 1, 2, 3, 4, and 5
>   (see pages 208–212)
>
> Card stock (optional)
>
> Magnetic or movable alphabet (optional)
>
> An empty bag or basket

ONE STEP AHEAD

Start with Build-a-Word Set 1. Print and cut out the photos and letters in this set. It is helpful to glue them to card stock for added durability. Children experience the most success with this activity if they already have some familiarity with letter names and sounds. There are many playful ways to review alphabet letters and sounds with your child, ranging from reading alphabet books together to playing alphabet "I Spy" while driving in the car: "I spy something that starts with the letter *b*."

THE PROCESS

Review the pictures and the corresponding words in Build-a-Word Set 1 with your child. Put the photos in a bag or a basket and place the letters face up on a table. Invite your child to choose a picture from the bag and then match the sounds she hears in the word with the letters she sees on the table. A helpful prompt is to ask your child what first (second, or last) sound she hears in the word. Make sure to overpronounce each sound: "What is the first sound you hear in c-a-t?"

> **Books to Inspire**
>
> *Word Wizard* by Cathryn Falwell

Once your child has lined up all three sounds in the word, in this case *cat,* ask her to point to each letter and say each sound, "c, a, t." Then encourage your child to run her finger across the entire word as she blends the sounds together, "cat."

Repeat this process for each Build-a-Word set or make your own set with your child.

MORE TO EXPLORE

Once your child has built the words in the Build-a-Word pictures, you can set aside the letters and invite her to choose a picture from the bag and write the word down on a sheet of paper.

WHERE IS THE SOUND?

Reading really starts coming together for children when they realize that distinct sounds can blend together to make words. This helps children solidify their knowledge of letter sounds and encourages them to listen closely and identify the separate phonemes of three-letter words.

ONE STEP AHEAD

Before engaging your child in this activity, make a chart with three pockets. Take a piece of card stock and fold up approximately one-third of the sheet (see the photo); then staple it in four places (the left side, the right side, and one-third of the way in from each side) to make three pockets. Next, prepare index cards by writing one letter of a three-letter word on each card.[3] Try to use words that contain sounds that your child already knows. Build-a-Word Set printables 1 through 5 are good resources for appropriate words to use for this experience.

THE PROCESS

Place the letter cards, one letter at a time, facedown in order in the pockets on your chart. Tell your child the word that the cards spell, such as *mat*, pronouncing it slowly and accentuat-

Materials

One piece of card stock paper

Blank index cards

A black pen

A stapler and staples

ing each sound. Next ask him to tell you where the "mmm" sound is in the word *mat*. "Is the mmm sound in the beginning, middle, or end of the word *mat*?" Encourage your child to check his answer by flipping over the card he guessed.

Repeat this process for each letter in the word, and then replace the cards with the letters for a new word.

MORE TO EXPLORE

You can use legal-size paper to make a game using four-letter words. With four-letter words you can explore vowel combinations (ea, ee, ie, ou, and so on) and digraphs (th, sh, ph, wh, and so on).

POETRY PUZZLES

Poetry puzzles offer an engaging experience that celebrates your child's favorite poems, nurtures a love of words, and encourages him to look closely at letters, sounds, words, punctuation, and how sentences are built.

ONE STEP AHEAD

Before engaging in this project with your child, spend some time reading poetry together. Revisit your child's favorite poems often. Once your child has grown fond of a particular poem, write it out on large strips of paper (one sentence per strip).

> **Materials**
>
> A favorite poem
>
> Long strips of blank paper
>
> A black pen
>
> A sentence holder or tabletop
>
> Scissors

THE PROCESS

Explain to your child that you have a special puzzle that you would like to show him. If he seems intrigued, tell him that rather than a typical picture puzzle, you have a poetry puzzle.

Start out by reading the poem you selected from the book and keep it nearby. Next, lay out the sentence strips and read the poem together again. Invite your child to mix up the sentence strips and then see if he can put the poem back together. Encourage your child to use the original poem as a reference.

After your child has mastered the sentence strips, you can extend the experience by inviting him to cut up the individual words for each sentence. It is helpful to do one sentence at a time. Some clues he can look for when putting together each sentence are capital letters to mark the beginning of the sentence and punctuation to mark the end of the sentence.

When your child is finished, store the puzzle pieces in an envelope so he can do it again at a later time.

MORE TO EXPLORE

A fun variation is to do the same activity with the words from a favorite song, a passage from a beloved book, or an inspiring quote.

> **Books to Inspire**
>
> *The Bill Martin Jr Big Book of Poetry* Edited by Bill Martin Jr. with Michael Sampson
>
> *Julie Andrews' Collection of Poems, Songs, and Lullabies* Selected by Julie Andrews and Emma Walton Hamilton

COLLECTING WORDS

Starting word collections is a wonderful way to generate enthusiasm and an appreciation for written
and spoken language. Word collections also help
to deepen your child's vocabulary, which benefits
both her reading and writing process.

ONE STEP AHEAD

Reading one of the stories mentioned in this section really helps to create enthusiasm for starting
word collections. Before starting this activity gather some interesting
children's magazines with age-appropriate language.

THE PROCESS

Invite your child to start her own word collection by cutting out some of
her favorite words from magazines. If your child loves cutting things out
of magazines as much as mine do, this should be an enticing invitation!

Books to Inspire

The Boy Who Loved Words
  by Roni Schotter

Max's Words by Kate
  Banks

*Sparkle and Spin: A Book
  about Words* by Ann
  and Paul Rand

Have your child start by cutting out any word that
strikes her fancy, and then another. Once a nice pile has
formed, you can encourage your child to put the words
into groups. Ask your child what types of categories she
can come up with for all of her words. For example,
my youngest daughter created a category of things she
loves. Once all of your child's words have been put into
distinct groups, she can paste them into her blank book
and write a label at the top of each page for the different categories.

Encourage your child to add to her collection over
time. Word collections make a wonderful resource for
young authors who are trying to spruce up their writing
by coming up with interesting language.

MORE TO EXPLORE

While initially your child's word collection will begin with categories such
as favorite things, places, and activities, as she gets older you can invite
her to create categories for nouns, adjectives, verbs, and more.

before she was able to identify what the number nine looked like. I would also like to note that children might repeat certain stages as they learn more advanced forms of mathematics. In other words, for every new concept that a child learns (addition, fractions, measurement, division, and so on), it is helpful for her to start with concrete hands-on experiences (Stage I) and build a solid understanding before moving on to a more abstract conceptualization of it (Stage III).[2] Children generally go through three stages of mathematical thinking as they learn new concepts and skills.

Stage I

Our youngest mathematicians live in the world of concrete thought. Their math and counting experiences should be grounded with real-life objects that that they can hold, sort, classify, and count.

Children in this stage are building number concepts on a variety of different levels. Because parents love to count with their young children, and because counting is incorporated into so many early childhood books and television shows, children learn the sequence of numbers much the same way they learn the words to a song. Simultaneously, children are beginning to recognize numbers and are learning the number names. Both of these are important skills for young children to master. During this time they also need to participate in playful hands-on math experiences so they can build one-to-one correspondence of numbers. One-to-one correspondence is a child's ability to associate one object with each number that is counted; that is, they can grasp that the number six represents six items. This may seem simple, but it is a big developmental milestone for children and an important building block.

The best way to support Stage I mathematicians is to provide a lot of fun experiences that include counting, sorting, classifying, and graphing objects from their everyday lives. Reading counting books together is also a great way to build number recognition and one-to-one correspondence. The simple act of pointing to one object at a time while reading or enjoying a math experience together helps children make the connection that each item counts as a different number and that the number you end with represents the number of items in a group.

Stage II

In Stage II, children begin to translate their concrete math experiences into more abstract symbols and problem solving.[3] During Stage II children may be frustrated because they are in a dance between the need for hands-on experiences and the ability to conceptualize how those experiences relate to abstract algorithms. It is this dance between the worlds of concrete and abstract thought that provides them with the conceptual understanding they need.

During this stage it can often feel like children take one step forward and two steps back. It is the resolution of this disequilibrium that results in solid mathematicians.[4] I have found with my own children that when they reach a level of frustration, it always helps to take them back to something concrete so they can visualize what they are trying to learn. If your child is working on an addition problem, for example, give him something that he can count out or a number line (see the Number Line printable on page 217) to work with. Also, don't underestimate the power of learning to count on your fingers. Fingers are helpful tools at this stage, and children should take full advantage of them. If your child is working with fractions, give him a cookie to divide. If he is working with measurement, take out a ruler, and so on and so forth.

Children become more agile with numbers at this stage and are ripe for some new challenges. Asking your child to help solve mathematical problems that come up in daily situations is a playful way to help develop his number sense. "We have five dollars and want to buy some apples that cost three dollars. Do we have enough money? How much will we have left over?" "We are having two friends over for a play date. They will each want two cookies. How many cookies do we need?" The goal is to increase your child's agility and flexibility with numbers so he can independently solve any of life's mathematical problems that come his way.

Stage III

If children have had adequate time to engage in hands-on mathematical experiences in stages I and II, they will thrive in Stage III. Children in Stage III have successfully crossed the bridge from concrete to abstract mathematical concepts and can effectively solve more traditional mathematical problems.[5] Our oldest daughter is in Stage III for her addition skills, yet she ventured back to Stage I as she started learning to tell time. After many months of using objects, number lines, and fingers to answer simple mathematical equations, she quickly went on to memorize her addition math facts. The important thing to note is that the memorization came to her quickly because she had gained a solid foundation in the principles behind addition through her explorations during stages I and II.

Now that your Stage III mathematician has the ability to deal with more abstract mathematical thinking, it is fun to keep her on her toes with more complex real-world problem solving. "We have six strawberries and three people. How many strawberries can each of us eat?" "If you have seven friends at your bowling party, how many bowling shoes do we need ask for?"

The projects that follow provide concrete and meaningful learning experiences that will expose your children to a variety of mathematical concepts. Be sure to always take your child's mathematical stage into consideration while demonstrating to her that math has fun and practical applications that can enhance her daily activities.

CLIP COUNTING

Clip counting offers a tactile experience that is hard for young children to resist. By leaving the materials out on a table or shelf, children, who are naturally curious, will want to engage with the project. This experience is great for developing number recognition, one-to-one correspondence, and knowledge of chronological order. Taking on and off the small clips is also wonderful for strengthening fine motor skills.

ONE STEP AHEAD

Before starting this activity, gather the materials. Print the Clip Math and Number Line printables on card stock; you can cover them with contact paper for extra durability.

Counting books are a wonderful way to introduce your child to the world of numbers.

Materials

Card stock

Small wooden clips (or paper clips)

Clip Math printable (see pages 213–216)

Number Line printable (see page 217)

Clear contact paper (optional)

Children love the intimate time spent in a loved one's lap, pointing to and counting the objects in their favorite books. Reading these books together helps to familiarize your child with numbers and counting, which will set the stage for success in the following activities.

THE PROCESS

For younger children you can start by simply setting out number cards and math clips on a table. When your child discovers this activity, encourage him to spread out all of the cards in numerical order across the table. Next, invite your child to start placing the clips on the appropriate cards.[6]

When he is finished putting clips on the cards, count the clips together, and then ask, "Does the number we counted match the number on the card?" If your child does not know all of his numbers yet, simply count the clips or dots out loud together and then point to the number and say, "This is the number ____."

Once your child is done with the activity, place it on a shelf where he can access it anytime he likes.

> **Books to Inspire**
>
> *Anno's Counting Book* by Mitsumasa Anno
>
> *Each Orange Had 8 Slices* by Paul Giganti Jr.
>
> *Over in the Meadow* by Olive A. Wadsworth
>
> *Teeth, Tails, and Tentacles: An Animal Counting Book* by Christopher Wormell
>
> *Ten, Nine, Eight* by Molly Bang

MORE TO EXPLORE

Once your child has solidified his one-to-one correspondence, he can expand his experience to incorporate addition and subtraction problems. Have him choose two numbers and attach the correct amount of clips. Then introduce the addition and equals symbols, explaining that the plus sign means how many clips there are altogether. Once he feels confident

writing the answer at the end of a math sentence, encourage him to write out an entire math equation. Have a number line handy so your child can double-check his answers and number formation.

BLACK-DOT ADVENTURES

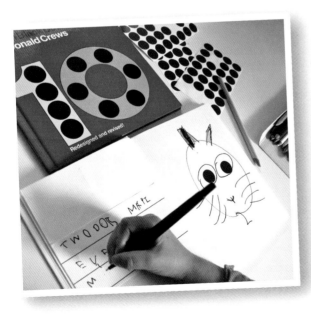

Black-dot adventures give children the opportunity to improve their number recognition, one-to-one correspondence, number sequencing, and number formation. It's wonderful—although not necessary—to read *Ten Black Dots* by Donald Crews before working on this activity. Having your child create a book of her own based on a well-known published book allows her to experience a sense of accomplishment and pride in writing like a real grown-up author. The whole family will thoroughly enjoy her finished product as a welcome addition to your home library. Of course this is a very fun and creative exercise on its own, so don't hesitate even if you don't have *Ten Black Dots* to read first.

ONE STEP AHEAD

Donald Crews is a great children's book author who has written a variety of charming books. Check out a few of his books from the library, and share them with your child before engaging in this experience. Already being a fan of Crews's books will make black-dot adventures even more meaningful for your child.

THE PROCESS

Read *Ten Black Dots* together with your child or explain that you'll be creating images that incorporate black dots. The story begins with the question, "What can you do with ten black dots?" and then goes on to show clever illustrations incorporating one through ten black dots in numerical order.

Just the sight of the black-dot stickers and a blank book should inspire your child to get busy making her black-dot creations. Invite your child to start by creating an image that incorporates one black dot.[7] Some examples may be a flower with a black-dot center, a sun, or a ball. From there have her create pictures that incorporate two, three, four, and up to ten black dots.

When your child is ready to write words to complement her drawings, add lines in her book to help guide her writing. It is also useful to have a number line and an alphabet chart available to help with correct letter and number formation. Young children may want to dictate their words for you to write down for them.

This is a fun activity to do with a sibling or on a playdate, because the exchange of ideas really inspires them.

Materials

A blank book (see pages 50–54)

Several ¾-inch black dot labels

A black felt-tip marker

Colored pencils

Number Line printable (see page 217)

Alphabet Chart printable (see page 197)

Books to Inspire

Fish Eyes: A Book You Can Count On by Lois Ehlert

Ten Black Dots by Donald Crews

MORE TO EXPLORE

Challenge your child to go beyond illustrations containing ten black dots. Explore ideas for numbers eleven through twenty.

COUNTING SEASHELLS BY THE SEASHORE

Providing your child with interesting materials with which she can explore and experiment is a great way to keep her engaged with mathematical concepts for increasingly longer periods of time. Counting seashells provides ample opportunity for a young mathematician to participate in math play on a variety of levels.

For young children, this experience offers a fun way to explore the mathematical concepts of developing one-to-one correspondence, number recognition, and accurate number sequencing. For children who are ready to transition from concrete mathematical activities to more abstract problem solving, this experience provides a playful way to introduce the concept of addition.

Materials

Sheets of sandpaper

Several 5 x 8 inch blue index cards

Seashells

Number Cards printable (see page 218)

Seashore Story Problems printable (see page 219)

Math Equations printable (see page 220)

Blank Math Equations printable (see page 221)

ONE STEP AHEAD

In preparation for this activity, cut ten island shapes out of sandpaper and glue them onto blue index cards. Next, print and cut out the Number Cards printable. For older mathematicians, print out Seashore Story Problems, Math Equations, and Blank Math Equations printables. It is always nice to have the materials prepared ahead of time and arranged in attractive containers. Displaying items in an aesthetically pleasing manner makes the activity that much more appealing to children. Keeping materials organized and easily accessible fosters independence and encourages children to take out and put away the materials themselves.

THE PROCESS

For young children in Stage I, start by spreading out the island cards in two rows of five on a large flat surface. Place the number cards in random order below the island cards.

Invite your child to count the number of islands and place the number cards in order below each one (for younger children you can do this step for them). Once your child has the numbers laid out in the correct sequence, encourage her to place the correct number of shells on each island to match the number below it.[8]

When your child is in Stage II and has solidified her number recognition and one-to-one correspondence, you can use the same materials to move her into more abstract problem solving. To start, provide your child with one of the island cards, a box of shells, and a basket with the Math Equations printable. Then encourage her to pick a problem and use the shells to help her solve the equation.

For your Stage III child, who already has some experience with addition problems, you can introduce him to the Seashore Story Problems. Provide him with a Blank Math Equations printable so he can write out his answers. It is also a great opportunity to demonstrate the use of a number line for addition as a way to check his work. Explain that he starts at the first number of an equation and then counts up the line the same number of spots as the second number of the equation. The number he lands on is the answer. Becoming comfortable with using a number line will really help your child as he begins to learn more formal addition and subtraction in school.

Books to Inspire

Over in the Ocean: In a Coral Reef by Marianne Berkes

Seashells by the Seashore by Marianne Berkes

Using children's collections such as seashells, pebbles, acorns, and so on offers many great opportunities for math experiences in sorting, counting, graphing, and more. Try using the same shells that you used in this activity to sort by color, size, and shape.

STACKING BEADS

Stacking beads is a simple yet fulfilling math activity that offers children a concrete experience, which develops number recognition and one-to-one correspondence and offers the opportunity to explore both addition and subtraction. The appeal of the materials makes this a hard-to-resist experience for children at all stages of their mathematical development.

Materials

Two large nails (without heads)

A rectangular piece of wood

Beads with large holes (that fit over the nails)

Math Equations printable (see page 220)

Blank Math Equations printable (see page 221)

Number Line printable (see page 217)

To prepare for this activity in advance, nail two large nails into a flat rectangular piece of wood (this is now a stacking board). Place some beads in an attractive container, and then simply leave the activity out for your child to discover. It is delightful to see how quickly children gravitate toward interesting and engaging materials.

Set out your new stacking board along with some beads and the Math Equations printable. Once your child has discovered the materials, let him freely explore them for a while.

When he seems to be ready for a challenge, invite your child to use the beads to solve the math problems that you've printed out. Encourage him to put the same number of beads as the first number in the math equation on the first nail and the second number on the second nail. Next have him add all of the beads together to come up with the correct answer.[9] For younger children it is helpful to do the first couple of equations together. It is also handy to have a number line close by to use as a model for correct number formation.

Encourage your child to make up his own math sentences using the Blank Math Equations printable. Challenge your child to investigate how many different ways he can make the number ten.

MORE TO EXPLORE

Explore the concept of subtraction by simply using one of the nails. Start with a number of beads on the nail. Then take several beads off of the nail. Ask your child how many are left. If your child shows an interest in taking subtraction further, demonstrate how to use a number line to double-check his answers. Start by finding the first (or largest) number on a number line and then count back the same number of spots as the second number. The number he lands on is the answer.

ADDING IT UP

Adding it up is a great transitional activity for moving from concrete mathematical skills to more abstract problem solving. While this activity provides practice with simple number recognition and one-to-one correspondence, it can be adapted to address the development of addition and subtraction skills as well.

> **Books to Inspire**
>
> *A String of Beads* by Margarette S. Reid
>
> *The Warlord's Beads* by Virginia Walton Pilegard

> **Materials**
>
> Number Cards printable (see page 218)
>
> Clear contact paper (optional)
>
> Manila shipping tags
>
> A variety of small stamps or stickers
>
> Magnetic adhesive tape (if done on a magnetic board)
>
> Magnetic hooks or clips (if done on a magnetic board)

ONE STEP AHEAD

Before engaging in this activity with your child, print and cut out the Number Cards printable. We used a magnetic board for this activity, so I covered the number cards with clear contact paper and attached magnetic adhesive tape to the back of them. You can also choose to use a large flat surface. It is helpful to prepare the tags ahead of time by putting small stamps or stickers (in different quantities from one to ten) on each card. For an extra challenge, create some tags with different combinations, such as three ladybugs plus four leaves (see the following photos).

THE PROCESS

For young mathematicians lay out number cards one through ten on a magnetic board or flat surface. Invite your child to choose one of your premade tags and place it under the corresponding number.[10]

Books to Inspire

Quack and Count by Keith Baker

Ten Flashing Fireflies by Philemon Sturges

Once your child has placed all of the cards in the correct locations, you can offer her a challenge by giving her cards that show combinations, such as three ladybugs plus two leaves, and ask her to put the tag under the number that shows how many items that tag has altogether.

For Stage III mathematicians you can create tags that have basic addition or subtraction problems, such as 2 + 3 =, 4 + 6 =, 5 − 4 =, or 3 − 1 =. It is important to only create addition equations that have answers of ten or less. Keep a number line handy so your child can double-check her work.

MORE TO EXPLORE

Once your young mathematician has crossed over to more abstract mathematical thinking, start posing math equations that arise in her daily life. "We have five cookies. How many will be left if you eat two?"

LET'S GRAPH IT

Children love to collect data. Introducing your child to the skill of creating and reading graphs offers him a wonderful way to organize and make sense of the information he gathers. Graphing common objects is a great way for children to learn mathematical concepts such as creating and

interpreting graphs, making predictions, and drawing conclusions. As you discuss your child's discoveries with him, you can also introduce him to valuable mathematical vocabulary such as greater than, less than, least, most, and fewer.

Materials

Collection of pebbles

My Pebble Graph printable (see page 222)

My Candy Graph printable (see page 223)

ONE STEP AHEAD

Print out the graph paper you plan to use ahead of time. When your child becomes interested, you will be graph ready!

THE PROCESS

For this activity, we used pebbles that we had collected one day during a visit to the beach. There is something special about using a child's personal collections for this activity; it increases his engagement and makes him truly interested in the results of the data. Use whatever collections you have on hand, substituting for the pebbles in these instructions.

Give your child the graph paper and ask him to place his pebbles, one by one, on the sheet in the appropriate spaces. As your child is working, you can ask him questions to help facilitate his thinking. Some examples are:

Which color stone do you have the most of?

Which color stone do you have the least of?

Which color stone do you have three of?

Who has the most orange stones? (If there is more than one child participating.)

Do you have an equal amount of stones of some colors?

How many white stones do you have?

How many gray stones do you have?

As you add stones to your graph, can you predict which stone you will have the most of? Least of?

How many more orange stones than gray stones do you have?

If you are doing this activity with more than one child, ask each of them to compare and contrast their results.

MORE TO EXPLORE

As a special variation on this activity, it can be a real treat to graph some candy! Sunspire SunDrops or M&M'S work well due to their size and color variations. Have your child merrily graph the contents of his bag of candy on his candy graph.

> **Books to Inspire**
>
> *Everybody Needs a Rock* by Byrd Baylor
>
> *If You Find a Rock* by Peggy Christian
>
> *On My Beach There Are Many Pebbles* by Leo Lionni

BELOVED BUTTONS: SORTING AND CLASSIFYING

Sorting and classifying objects helps children strengthen their logical and analytical skills. This activity is a great example of how literature can be used to inspire mathematical thinking in young children. Through this experience children are also introduced to mathematical vocabulary terms such as group, set, more than, less than, and equal to.

ONE STEP AHEAD

An interesting collection of buttons will really enhance this experience. You can either gather a button collection beforehand or do so over time with your children. Print out the Sorting and Classifying printables and have them at the ready for this project.

THE PROCESS

A great book to introduce this experience is *The Button Box* by Margarette S. Reid. It is a captivating story about a young boy who loves his grandmother's collection of buttons. After reading the book you can tell your child that you have something special for him and present him with his very own button collection. If you don't read the book, the button collection on its own should inspire some creative fun.

Give your child some time to examine his newly acquired collection. After some free exploration, choose two buttons and ask your child to tell you something that is the same or different about them.[11] Most likely your child will name some attributes of the buttons, such as how many holes they have, their size, their color, or their texture.

Next you can ask your child, "If you were going to put your buttons into groups, what groups would you make?" Supply your child with blank cards so he can label the categories he would like to create.

After your child has finished sorting his buttons based on his first set of categories, ask if he can come up with a different way to sort the buttons and repeat the process.

It is fun to rotate the Sorting and Classifying printables your child uses based on the number of categories he comes up with. After a couple of rounds, encourage your child to choose the appropriate sheet to use.

Materials

Assortment of buttons

Small index cards cut in half or plain paper for labeling categories

Sorting and Classifying printables, 1–3 (see pages 224–226)

Books to Inspire

The Button Box by Margarette S. Reid

Grandma's Button Box by Linda Williams Aber

Sorting by Henry Arthur Pluckrose

Encourage your child to sort his button collection by different attributes, such as color, size, shape, and any other characteristics he may notice. My girls decided to sort buttons that have "swirls" and buttons with "no swirls."

PATTERNS EVERYWHERE

Identifying and understanding patterns is a critical skill for mathematicians. Our world is full of beautifully breathtaking patterns; once a child begins to develop an eye for recognizing them, there is no holding back the connections she can make.

ONE STEP AHEAD

It is fun to choose a colorful, inexpensive photo album for this project. For my girls, the newness of the "book" they were using added to the project's intrigue.

To take your child's thinking about patterns to the next level, spend some time on the Pattern Wizardry Web site by the Brooklyn Children's Museum. They have a wonderful teacher's guide that outlines learning experiences for different kinds of patterns. The types of patterns they list are: linear, symmetry, branching, spirals, and tessellations.

Materials

A small photo album or blank book

A camera

Types of Patterns printable (see page 227)

THE PROCESS

Pattern by Henry Arthur Pluckrose and *Lots and Lots of Zebra Stripes: Patterns in Nature* by Stephen R. Swinburne are great entry points for introducing children to the concept of patterns. After reading and discussing the books with your child, encourage her to look around your yard and take pictures of any patterns she discovers. I was amazed to see how seriously my daughters took their pattern search; they were focused on the task for a long time and took almost a hundred pictures (thank goodness for digital photos!).

Print the photos that your child took—or a selection of her photos—and invite her to create her very own pattern book.

Before placing your child's pattern pictures in her book, introduce her to the Types of Patterns printable. Then ask your child if she can figure out which category each of her photos fits into. Once your child has

categorized all of her pattern photographs, she can put them into her pattern book along with a label to identify each kind of pattern.

To this day my girls are still noticing patterns around them. Whenever they have a question about the kind of pattern something may be, they have their very own pattern books to use as a reference.

Books to Inspire

Lots and Lots of Zebra Stripes: Patterns in Nature by Stephen R. Swinburne

Pattern by Henry Arthur Pluckrose

WEB SITES TO INSPIRE

Pattern Wizardry by Brooklyn Children's Museum, www.brooklyn kids.org/patternwizardry

MORE TO EXPLORE

Add to your child's exploration of patterns by having her attribute letters or numbers to patterns she sees. For example, a striped pattern of red, blue, green, red, blue, green could become an ABCABC pattern or a 123123 pattern. Ask your child if she can predict and draw a picture of what comes next.

MEASURING OUR WORLD

Learning to measure our world is a welcome experience for young children. I always loved the excitement in the classroom during our measurement units. Children love being able to use "real tools" to measure things that they encounter on a daily basis. This experience will introduce your child to both standard and nonstandard measurement and help him to develop the important skill of estimation.

Materials

One small LEGO (approximately one inch)

A clipboard (optional)

A ruler

A 12 x 2 inch piece of paper

LEGO Measurements printable (see page 228)

Body Measurements printable (see page 229)

ONE STEP AHEAD

Having all the materials printed and prepared in advance for this project helps with the activity's overall flow. The steps outlined do not need to happen all at the same time, so plan for this project to take place in stages on different occasions.

THE PROCESS

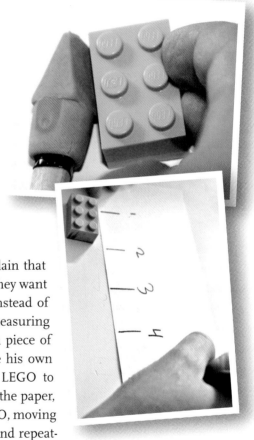

Start with a small LEGO (approximately one inch) and the LEGO Measurements printable. Ask your child to hunt around the house and see how many items he can find that are approximately the same length as the LEGO. If you have one available, give your child a clipboard; it makes the search that much more "official." Encourage your child to record his discoveries on the measurement sheet.

When your child is finished, explain that grown-ups do the same thing when they want to know how long an item is, but instead of using LEGOs they use rulers or measuring tapes. Next, take out the 12 x 2 inch piece of paper and invite your child to make his own ruler. Explain that he can use his LEGO to make marks (starting at one edge of the paper, making a mark after placing his LEGO, moving it forward to the edge of the mark, and repeating, all they way to the end of the sheet). When he is finished marking and numbering his ruler, take out one of your rulers and show your child how similar they are. He may notice that both rulers have twelve spaces. Tell him that on rulers those spaces are called inches. You can also tell him that twelve inches makes one foot.

It not important that your child's measurements be exact. What is important is that he begins to create mental images of items that are *approximately* an inch long. This will help him tremendously when it comes to estimating measurements and will give him the internal mechanism for knowing whether his results are in the ballpark.

Once your child's handmade ruler is complete, encourage him to put his new tool to work. Suggest that he measure the various parts of his body (it is nice to work with a part-

ner for this part of the experience) and write his findings on the Body Measurements printable. Explain that he can start by estimating how long an item will be, such as an ear, then measure the item, and finish by trying to figure out how far off his estimate was from his measurement.

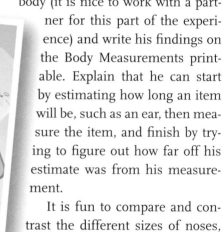

It is fun to compare and contrast the different sizes of noses, fingers, and so on among your family members.

MORE TO EXPLORE

After your child is comfortable measuring items by the inch, you can repeat the same process with the smallest LEGO piece (see the bottom of the LEGO measurements printable), introducing the centimeter as another unit of measurement.

Challenge your child to measure longer items with the use of a cloth or metal tape measure (keep an eye out for hurt fingers with the metal tape measure) or yardstick.

> **Books to Inspire**
>
> *Inch by Inch* by Leo Lionni
>
> *Me and the Measure of Things* by Joan Sweeney
>
> *Measuring Penny* by Loreen Leedy

4 Scientific Investigations

Those who contemplate the beauty of the earth find reserves of strength that will endure as long as life lasts.

— Rachel Carson

Seeing the natural world through the eyes of a child is an enlightening phenomenon. Their innate appreciation of and fascination for all living things are qualities that can lead to many fulfilling learning experiences. The universe provides parents with unlimited opportunities for connecting with their children. Whether you are examining a grain of sand, veins on a leaf, or the parts of a flower, all it takes is some time spent together in the great outdoors and an attitude of inquiry to make the world come alive with infinite possibilities for discovery.

The following developmental overview will help guide the scientific explorations you share with your child. It's amazing how the right bit of information presented at the right time can open up a whole new world.

Developmental Overview

Stage I

Starting at a very young age children begin to build their own theories about the way the world works. These theories are constructed through their hands-on experiences and are constantly evolving based on new discoveries. Although these early theories may not be scientifically correct, they reveal a thought process that parents can carefully guide to more accurate conclusions about the world. It is important that a child's early theories be heard and understood, rather than corrected. This does not mean that you withhold relevant facts from your child, because even young children love to know the "right answer." When possible it is best to *show* your child rather than to *tell* her how things really work. Young scientists learn best through direct experience. At this early stage, developing an attitude of inquiry is essential for children—the scientific facts and accuracy will come with time.

Children in Stage I are naturally curious. Their inquisitive nature provides ample opportunities for parents to transform their questions into meaningful learning experiences. All it takes is a magnifying glass and an empty container for collecting treasures to transform an ordinary day at the park into an adventurous scientific exploration. Let your child's questions and interests lead your investigations. If she becomes fascinated by a certain topic, build on your outdoor experiences by taking a trip to the library together to "do research."

During this stage I highly recommend hands-on activities. Have your child cut open a flower, tear apart a leaf, look inside an acorn, let a worm crawl around on her hand, study a single blade of grass, feed your backyard birds—demonstrate to your child that there is always more to what she sees.

The art of noticing leads to fascinating discoveries. Take time to help your child notice the little things, which we often overlook in our busy grown-up lives. Simple things like the clouds moving, the colors of a sunset, the shape of the moon, or the squirrel in your front yard are enchanting to a young child. Notice how things in the natural world change over time—look at the same flower every day, watch the changing leaves on your favorite tree, or track the time the sun sets for several days. Sharing these moments with your child encourages her to develop an awareness and appreciation for the world around her.

Collecting is another activity that is inherently pleasing to young children and makes for fun family time together. One of our favorite family activities is searching for pebbles together at a nearby beach. It is a deeply satisfying experience for all of us; nothing else seems to matter when you are looking for that just-right rock, and nothing compares to the thrill of sharing your discoveries with the ones you love. Some of our other cherished collections consist of leaves, acorns, shells, pressed flowers, and seeds. Save your family's collections and then use them for a variety of sorting activities. As you review your bounty upon returning home, take out a few bowls and ask your child to organize her collection. This can lead to interesting conversations as your child learns to come up with ways to categorize what she has found.

For children at every age it is beneficial to talk about the connections between things. Too many of us only learned about science from the two-dimensional world of textbooks. We learned a sequence of facts about a variety of topics in a linear progression. Yet we do not live in a two-dimensional world, and science is filled with multidimensional relationships that cannot be fully understood or appreciated through the memorization of disjointed facts. Parents can point out the connections between all living things and talk about the important role that each one plays in the web of life. Children intuitively understand this relatedness and listen to stories about the natural world with the same anticipation as they have for a bedtime tale. You do not need to be a scientific expert, and there is a lot that you will learn with your children as you go; simply remember to look for opportunities to connect your child's object of interest with a cycle, a season, a food chain, or another living thing. When children begin to internalize the interconnectedness of all life, they will become more aware of the important role that humans play and hopefully more conscious of the impact they are making in the world.

When you engage your children in this attentive manner, it teaches them to dig deeper, look longer, and seek out more information—all of their own volition. By providing your young scientists with plenty of time outdoors and simple scientific tools (see "Playful Learning Spaces"), you are sending them a powerful message that their questions matter and that behind a simple question there is a universe full of interesting and sometimes even magical things.

Stage II

Stage II is marked by a child's ability to notice, talk about, and document the finer points of the natural world. These children are beginning to discover and identify aspects of things that they have always admired but did not notice in detail before, such as the veins on a leaf, the texture of bark, or the patterns on a shell. By identifying more specific attributes of interesting objects, Stage II scientists are building the necessary knowledge for more elaborate scientific investigations. What started out as simple collections in Stage I can now be sources for lessons in classification. Your child's beloved seashell or rock collection takes on new meaning, as Stage II scientists are ready to differentiate various types of items by size, shape, color, and so on. Field guides take on more importance during this phase as children love to look up unidentified objects. Although your child is growing more interested in accuracy, scientific names may come and go during his inquiries. The goal during this stage is not the memorization of names and facts; rather, it is to nurture your child's intrinsic desire to pursue a topic with sustained focus for prolonged periods of time.

As your child gets older and more experienced in his worldly explorations, you can encourage a more systematic approach to his investigations. Providing journals for your child to record his observations and bringing along simple field guides on outings gives a Stage II scientist the resources he needs to take his understanding to the next level. During this stage you can also start to make the scientific process (see "Scientific Process" in "Printables" on page 230) more explicit. Even young children can be informally introduced to scientific concepts such as hypothesis, experiment, research, and making conclusions when they are used in the context of engaging pursuits. Here are some simple ways to incorporate these words into your everyday activities.

- When your child asks you a question, you can reply by asking him to make a "hypothesis."
- Use the word *research* as you look through informational books together or try to answer your child's questions. If your child asks a question that you do not have an answer for, you can reply by saying, "I am not sure, we should do some research."
- After talking about and spending some time on a particular topic, you can ask your child what "conclusions" he can make.

An early introduction and authentic use of these terms helps your child tackle questions using a more systematic approach. As he grows older, using the scientific method will come naturally to him as he encounters more advanced experiments and research questions.

During this stage be sure to talk about the work that scientists do and start using the word *science* in relation to the activities your child is pursuing. If children view themselves as scientists at a young age and start to connect their positive early experiences with "doing science," it will serve them well during more formal science classes in their school settings. With a good foundation, your child can move into this next phase feeling sure of his abilities and enthusiastic about the potential of scientific studies.

Stage III

With many self-initiated scientific explorations under their belts, Stage III scientists are ready to take on the world! Their earlier informal investigations and introduction to the scientific process have set the stage for more in-depth activities. It is a good time to share the scientific process (see "Scientific Process" in "Printables" on page 230) with your child and to let her know that most of the scientists in the world use a similar approach when trying to answer questions or discover new things.

It is helpful to introduce your child to the scientific process in steps. I started out by using a simple approach with my girls. I put together a handmade science journal containing sheets of paper that encouraged them to make a hypothesis when they had a question or wanted to investigate something, and an additional space for them to add any conclusions they made during the process (see "Science Journal 1" in "Printables" on page 231).

Once your child is comfortable making hypotheses and conclusions, you can add sheets that include more of the scientific process (see "Science Journal 2" in "Printables" on page 232). Simply leave them out with your child's science supplies or create special books for specific projects. Children love feeling as though they are doing the work of "real scientists" and appreciate the structure that the scientific process provides.

As with all the suggestions in this book, remember that this approach should never be pushed on a child. I leave our science journals in our atelier and let the girls use them when they want to. I may suggest that they

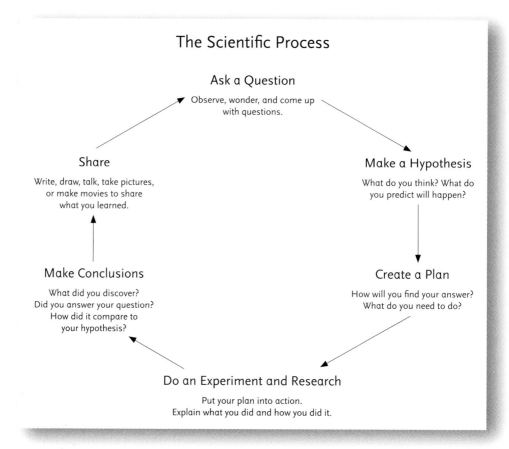

The Scientific Process

Ask a Question
Observe, wonder, and come up
with questions.

Share
Write, draw, talk, take pictures,
or make movies to share
what you learned.

Make a Hypothesis
What do you think? What do
you predict will happen?

Make Conclusions
What did you discover?
Did you answer your question?
How did it compare to
your hypothesis?

Create a Plan
How will you find your answer?
What do you need to do?

Do an Experiment and Research
Put your plan into action.
Explain what you did and how you did it.

use their science journals if they come up with a particular question they want to investigate, but if they are not interested, that is perfectly okay. Sometimes they just want to look at bug for the sake of looking at a bug!

Another great characteristic of Stage III scientists is their enthusiasm for naming things in the world. They take pride in using their classification skills to fully utilize their field guides. Make field guides readily available to your children by putting them in baskets or on low-level bookshelves; you never know when that bird, bug, or flower will appear that needs immediate attention! It is also fun to take field guides on the go. We have gotten into the habit of grabbing field guides on our way out the door—a leaf guide for the park, a shell guide for the beach, a bird guide for a hike, and so on. On these excursions I usually leave the books out (on the sand or grass), and more often than not the girls put them to good use.

Below is a list of some of our favorite field guides:

A *Golden Guide* series published by St. Martin's Press

Fandex Family Field Guides published by Workman Publishing Company

National Audubon Society First Field Guides published by Scholastic

Peterson First Guides published by Houghton Mifflin Harcourt

At this stage children are able retain many of the facts and names they learn and are delighted to share their newfound knowledge with friends and loved ones. With a little support and the right resources, Stage III scientists are ready to shoot for the moon!

The following learning experiences will foster an appreciation for the natural world. By slowing down and taking a closer look at the world around us, your child will see the extraordinary in the ordinary things that she might regularly pass by.

TERRARIUMS: A GLIMPSE INTO THE WATER CYCLE

Building and observing a terrarium together is a great way for children to better understand the water cycle. Learning about each part of the cycle and seeing it happen in his own little microcosm help to bring abstract concepts to life. You can use this learning experience to explore more advanced ideas from the physical sciences, such as how matter changes to different states: liquid (water) to gas (vapor) and to a solid (snow).

This activity also lends itself nicely to a discussion of our water supply—the fact that all of our water comes from the same source and is part of one big water cycle. A fun question to raise with your child is, "Did you know that the water you are drinking right now may have previously flowed down a stream in Thailand?" Just like the water in your terrarium recycles itself over and over again, so does the water on our planet. Once your child really grasps how the water cycle works, he will understand that our water supply is a resource that needs to be protected.

Materials

A large glass jar with an airtight lid

Small pebbles

Activated charcoal (can be found in the fish tank section of pet stores)

Soil (do not use potting soil if you want to try creating a habitat out of your terrarium)

One or two terrarium-friendly plants (Hypoestes, African violets, ferns, and other tropical plants)

Rocks, shells, or mementos for decoration

A small spray bottle

The Water Cycle printable (see page 233)

ONE STEP AHEAD

Some handy terms to know before diving into this project are:

Evaporation: When the sun heats up water from lakes, oceans, ponds, or puddles, it turns into vapor and rises in the air.

Transpiration: When moisture moves through plants from the roots to the leaves, it changes into vapor and is released into the air.

Condensation: When vapor gets cold, it turns back into water, which makes clouds.

Precipitation: When clouds get heavy with water, it starts to rain or snow.

THE PROCESS

Building a terrarium is a project that brings both long- and short-term satisfaction. While the initial process is fun, watching the terrarium over time can be fascinating. We leave our terrarium out on the kitchen counter, and it often finds its way into our daily conversations and musings.

To set up your terrarium, have your child place a layer of pebbles on the bottom of your jar approximately one inch deep. Sprinkle a thin layer of activated charcoal over the pebbles and then add a layer of soil about one to two inches deep. We used soil from our backyard so that we could spend some time exploring all the elements within the dirt and because we thought that we might eventually introduce some insects and worms into our terrarium, which would not do well in potting soil.

Place your plant(s) in the desired location and cover the roots with soil. Have your child add rocks, shells, or any other decorative items he chooses to personalize your terrarium. Finish off with a few sprays of water directly onto the soil and secure the lid to the jar.

After a day or so, your family will observe condensation building on the walls of the jar and notice precipitation as the drips of water

Books to Inspire

Down Comes the Rain by Franklyn M. Branley

A Drop around the World by Barbara Shaw McKinney

A Drop of Water: A Book of Science and Wonder by Walter Wick

A Kid's Guide to Making a Terrarium by Stephanie Bearce

One Well: The Story of Water on Earth by Rochelle Strauss

Terrarium Habitats by Kimi Hosoume and Jacqueline Barber

Water Dance by Thomas Locker

come back down to the soil. Leave out the Water Cycle printable to help your child identify each phase within your terrarium. If you keep the lid closed securely, you will only need to add a few sprays of water each week to keep your terrarium moist.

MORE TO EXPLORE

To help children better understand the role that plants play in the water cycle, cut a few fresh leaves from a plant and place them in a sealed plastic bag.[1] Tape the bag on a window overnight, and in the morning your child will find evidence of transpiration (drops of water within the bag).

Terrariums offer a unique glimpse into ecosystems and how they work. If you have used soil from your backyard, you can introduce worms, sow bugs, and pill bugs into your family's terrarium and then have your child observe the role they play in maintaining the soil. If you do decide to add living creatures to your terrarium, make sure that you add holes to the lid of your jar and water a little more frequently. A wonderful resource that can help guide you through this process while maintaining the utmost respect for the lives you are observing is *Terrarium Habitats* by Kimi Hosoume and Jacqueline Barber.

CAPTURING THE MOON

Creating moon journals together as a family is a great way to foster an appreciation for the natural world. By observing and recording the moon every few days, children learn how to document change over time, become familiar with cycles in nature, and develop an understanding of the relationship between the moon, the sun, and the earth. This activity also inspires a sense of being connected to something larger than oneself.

Materials

A blank journal (see page 50)

A variety of pencils and pens (if using dark paper, gel pens and light-colored pencils work best)

Flashlights

Phases of the Moon printable (see page 234)

ONE STEP AHEAD

Looking up the times of the moonrise and moonset in a farmer's almanac can be fun for the whole family. If you do this in the morning before making an observation, it will build anticipation as you wait for just the right time to go outside and look at the sky. A great Web site to explore together is www.almanac.com/moon.

A couple of handy facts to have under your belt when you begin your moon watching adventures are: When the moon appears to be getting smaller, it is referred to as waning. And when the moon appears to be getting larger, it is referred to as waxing.

THE PROCESS

There are few things in life as constant as seeing the moon at night, yet what seems most predictable about the moon is the cycle of change that it experiences month after month. Children are naturally curious about the moon and the mystique that it holds, which makes it a great entry point for learning about cycles in nature and how to observe change over time.

A nice way to introduce your children to this learning experience is by reading inspiring fiction and nonfiction children's books first (see "Books to Inspire" for our favorites). Check out a few moon-related books from the library and have them on hand. I used bedtime reading to introduce the girls to many of the books that I had gathered.

During conversations inspired by your reading together, look for an opening to introduce the idea of starting a moon journal. Once your child becomes intrigued by the idea, gather your materials in one spot so they are easily accessible each night. We used a basket to hold all of our moon books, journals, pens, pencils, and flashlights. We kept the basket near our front door so we could grab them on a moment's notice.

As a family, go outside after dark every few nights to document the moon's phase and talk about what you notice. Have your child create observational drawings in her moon journal of what she sees in the sky. Your child's sketches don't need to be limited to the moon. We snuck in some drawings of our favorite constellations, the clouds, and even some neighborhood trees. There were a few nights when the moon was not visible, so we simply drew what we saw.

When the time is right, you can introduce vocabulary associated with the phases of the moon, such as new moon, first quarter moon, full moon, third quarter moon, waxing, waning, gibbous, and crescent (see "Phases of the Moon" in "Printables" on page 234). You will be amazed at how quickly your child incorporates her newly acquired vocabulary into her drawings.

As time goes on, you can suggest that your child integrate different mediums into her moon journal, such as poetry, collage, paints, chalk, and more. We documented one full moon cycle. We still keep our moon journals handy and continue to do moon observations whenever the mood strikes.

It is important to note that both of my girls did not always want to go outside to record the moon on the same evenings. In an effort to keep this project playful, participation was always optional. The variety in their attendance provided us with some special one-on-one time with our daughters, which was a welcome bonus. At the end of the month both girls gained new insight into the phases of the moon. Spending time together observing nature and talking about our discoveries was a wonderful way to connect as a family.

Books to Inspire

FICTION

And If the Moon Could Talk by Kate Banks

Hello, Harvest Moon by Ralph Fletcher

Owl Moon by Jane Yolen

Papa, Please Get the Moon for Me by Eric Carle

NONFICTION

The Moon Seems to Change by Franklyn M. Branley

Moon Journals by Joni Chancer and Gina Rester-Zodrow

The Moon Book by Gail Gibbons

The Moon Book: A Lunar Pop-Up Celebration by Arlene Seymour

See also the Resources section

Web Site to Inspire

The Old Farmer's Almanac, www.almanac.com/moon

MORE TO EXPLORE

Once your child has learned the phases of the moon, it is interesting to explore its connection to the ocean tides.

CLOUD GAZING

For young scientists, cloud gazing, watching huge clouds gracefully dance across the sky, evokes an awesome sense of wonder. I will never forget the first time, as a child, when I realized clouds move and change shape, and it was wonderful to be there when my daughters had the same

epiphany. Stage II and Stage III scientists can begin to identify the types of clouds they see and start to make connections between cloud formations and weather.

Materials

Free time and a sky full of interesting clouds

A camera (optional)

Colored markers (optional)

Cloud formations (see Cloud Formations in Printables on page 235)

ONE STEP AHEAD

Aside from using your imagination to identify animals, shapes, and favorite objects within cloud formations, it is helpful to know the three basic types of clouds.

Cirrus clouds: High in the sky and are thin and wispy, looking a bit like feathers

Cumulus clouds: Low in the sky and look like fluffy cotton balls. They have distinct edges and often change shapes

Stratus clouds: Low lying, and often look like a big blanket across the sky

THE PROCESS

Slowing down and taking the time to watch the clouds go by is a great way to spend the afternoon. The good news is that it is free and needs little to no preparation.

Simply go outside, find a nice spot, and look up. Laying flat on your back in a nice patch of grass or on a blanket makes for a relaxing and memorable experience.

See how many shapes, objects, or animals your family can identify within the cloud formations. When appropriate, introduce the names of various cloud formations and see if your child can identify them.

To take this activity further, invite your child to take a photo or have your child draw a sketch of the clouds he sees. Looking at the photo or sketch later, ask your child if he can draw the objects he saw in the clouds with a colored pen or pencil (to incorporate a bit of technology, you can also use the drawing tool in a photograph editing program). Have your child label the types of clouds in the sky in your drawing or photo.

MORE TO EXPLORE

Once your child is able to identify the three basic cloud formations, you can introduce him to a greater variety of types of clouds. Encourage your child to make his own cloud guide by adding new pictures or sketches with each new identification. Cloud explorations also lend themselves nicely to making connections between different types of weather and the water cycle.

Books to Inspire

The Book of Clouds by John A. Day

The Cloud Book by Tomie dePaola

The Cloudspotter's Guide: The Science, History, and Culture of Clouds by Gavin Pretor-Pinney

It Looked Like Spilt Milk by Charles G. Shaw

Peterson First Guides: Clouds and Weather by John A. Day and Vincent J. Schaefer

THE LIFE CYCLE OF A SEED

No matter how many times I do this activity, whether it is with toddlers or grown-ups, I am always in awe of the power and determination of the seed to bring forth new life. Witnessing the process of the radicle breaking through the seed coat, taking root, and flourishing is a wonderful way to explore the cycle of life with your children.

Watching a simple bean seed sprout offers your child the opportunity to observe and document change over time. As the bean goes through its changes, your child can witness a plant's life cycle and identify its various parts as the new plant unfolds before his very eyes.

Materials

Bean seeds

A clear glass jar

Paper towels

Water

Parts of a Bean
Seed printable
(see page 236)

ONE STEP AHEAD

Along with referencing the Parts of a Bean Seed printable, some helpful vocabulary terms that can be introduced as each part of the bean plant presents itself are:

Seed coat: The outer layer that protects the seed

Cotyledon: The part of the seed that stores food for early growth

Radicle: The part of the plant that evolves into a root

Hypocotyl: The part of the seed that becomes a stem and helps to push the first leaves above ground

First true leaves: The first leaves to emerge from the seedling and the sign that photosynthesis is beginning for the plant

Primary root: The first root to emerge from the seedling. The primary root grows downward. The functions of both the primary and secondary roots are to anchor the plant to the ground, to absorb water and minerals from the soil, and to store food.

Secondary roots: Roots that emerge after the primary root and grow out to the sides

THE PROCESS

Dampen several paper towels, roll them up, and insert them into your glass jar. Make sure that the paper towels are thick enough to place sufficient pressure on the side of the jar to hold up a bean seed.

Place one to three bean seeds between the glass of your jar and the damp paper towels, leaving an inch or two above and below the seed for the roots and stem to grow. We first used adzuki bean seeds because that

---

Books to Inspire

From Seed to Plant by Allan Fowler

From Seed to Plant by Gail Gibbons

Grow Great Grub: Organic Food from Small Spaces by Gayla Trail

One Bean by Anne Rockwell

Seeds by Ken Robbins

Seeds! Seeds! Seeds! by Nancy Elizabeth Wallace

was what we had handy. Since then we have used a number if different bean seeds, all with equal success.

Place the jar in a sunny spot, and have your child watch nature take its course!

MORE TO EXPLORE

Adzuki beans display hypogeal germination, where the cotyledons stay in the ground. Other beans, such as green beans, have epigeal germination, where the cotyledons come out of the ground. It is fun to sprout a variety of beans so your family can compare and contrast the different types of germination.

This activity is a tried-and-true classroom favorite. You can add a valuable dimension to this experience by simultaneously planting the same type of bean seeds in a garden or a container. As your child watches his garden grow, the bean seed in the jar offers a behind-the-scenes look at what is happening under the soil outside. It is wonderful for children to experience the process of growing something from seed and seeing it through maturation until it reaches the dinner table.

DISSECTING FLOWERS

Discovering the hidden parts that exist within a flower can seem magical to children. Dissecting flowers is a quintessential opportunity for showing your child that there is always more to the natural world than meets the eye. We all know how special it is to take time to smell the flowers, and your child's in for an even bigger treat when you take a few extra moments to investigate what lies within them.

This learning experience inspires a sense of awe and appreciation for the natural world. It teaches children how to use scientific tools to identify and label different parts of a flower, compare and contrast different types of flowers, and learn about the reproductive cycle of a flower.

Materials

Freshly cut flowers

A magnifying glass

Child-sized knife and scissors

A cutting board

Parts of a Flower printables 1 and 2 (see pages 237–238)

ONE STEP AHEAD

Flowers are a plant's reproductive parts. You can prepare for this activity by learning a bit about pollination. The wind and various insects, such as bees and butterflies, play an important role in the life cycle of flowers. As insects fly from flower to flower in search of nectar, they collect pollen from the tip of the stamens, which are called anthers. When the pollen makes it to the stigma, it travels down the style into the ovary and fertilizes the ovules, thus producing new seeds.

THE PROCESS

This learning experience is most effective if you follow your child's lead and introduce it on a day she is naturally drawn to flowers. While she is picking a bouquet or making flower soup, for example, you can ask her if she has ever seen what is inside a flower. Once her interest is piqued, you can invite her to dissect some flowers.

Be sure to pick a variety of local flowers. Daffodils are a great choice because they have typical parts that are easy to find and label.

Allow your child time to freely explore (without an agenda) the flowers using a magnifying glass and tools for cutting. After she has had time to investigate (and tear apart) a flower, ask her if she found anything that looked like different *parts* of the flower. If her flower has already been dissected into little pieces, you can give her the Parts of a Flower 1 printable. She may want to start with a fresh flower, which is fine as well. If she is starting fresh, give her the Parts of a Flower 2 printable and suggest that she start by cutting the flower in half. Go ahead and join in; it's great fun to sit next to your child and dissect a flower of your own!

Some of the most exciting parts of a flower to discover are the ovules, which look like tiny little clear eggs and can usually be found in a bulb-like shape where the stem and the petals come together. Don't end your flower dissecting without uncovering the ovules!

> **Books to Inspire**
>
> *The Life Cycle of a Flower* by Molly Aloian and Bobbie Kalman
>
> *Pick, Pull, Snap! Where Once a Flower Bloomed* by Lola M. Schaefer
>
> *The Reason for a Flower* by Ruth Heller

Once your child has successfully identified the parts of one flower, encourage her to find the same parts on a variety of flowers.

Stage III scientists may like to record their findings by taping the parts they have identified to a piece of paper and writing labels for the names.

MORE TO EXPLORE

Once your child has identified the parts of a flower, you can explore the life cycle of flowers. When you introduce the role that birds, bees, and other insects play in the reproduction of a flower, the busy buzz of your garden will take on new meaning for your child as she begins to witness firsthand the connection between all living things.

ON THE SEASHORE

Focusing observations on one small, square space of land encourages children to take more time and look more closely at what they might ordinarily ignore. By choosing one specific area to explore, in this case at the beach, your child will make new discoveries and see the relationships between them.

I must admit that this experience was an eye-opener for me. As I walked the beach with my girls looking for a good spot to mark out our square spaces, I started to worry that the beach we had chosen did not have enough "stuff" on its shore. The girls took the lead and chose their spots, which upon first glance seemed to just contain seaweed. Once we settled in, we were astounded at the diversity of sea treasures that we found. A whole world opened up for us within those small spaces, and the same can happen for you and your family.

> ## Materials
>
> Four wooden rulers
>
> Wood glue
>
> A magnifying glass
>
> A seashore field guide
>
> A shovel for digging
>
> A bucket or containers for collecting
>
> A nature journal to record observations (optional)

ONE STEP AHEAD

Because every coast is unique, it is helpful to have a field guide that is specific to your area. There are some great laminated, foldable guides that are easy to slip into your bag. Our favorite seashore guide is *Beachcomber's Guide to the North Atlantic Seashore* published by the Massachusetts Audubon Society. You can also find a nice selection of portable guides at www.foldingguides.com.

THE PROCESS

Create your square for viewing a space by gluing four rulers together at the corners. Once the glue has completely dried, your square is ready for an adventure at the seashore.

Encourage your child to select a special spot that he would like to investigate. Have him place his square over his spot and then notice what he sees.

Start by exploring all the items on the surface of the sand. Have a bucket or container nearby so your child can set aside objects he would like to research at a later time. Having a field guide nearby helps with identifying new discoveries.

Once your child has skimmed the surface, suggest that he dig deeper within his square space to see if he can find anything else of interest. Don't forget to notice the variety of each type of object found—even within the grains of sand.

After your child has thoroughly explored the world within his small square space, if you have not done so already, spend some time together flipping through your field guides to identify some of the objects he chose to set aside. If you brought a nature journal, have fun making some observational drawings to help document and commemorate the moment.

When your investigation is finished, have your child return all of his seashore treasures back to the space in which he found them.

Books to Inspire

Beachcomber's Guide to the North Atlantic Seashore by the Massachusetts Audubon Society

One Small Square: Seashore by Donald M. Silver

Peterson First Guides: Seashores by John C. Kricher

Sand by Ellen J. Prager

The Seashore by Gallimard Jeunesse, Elisabeth Cohat, and Pierre De Hugo

Seashore Life: A Guide to Animals and Plants Along the Beach by Herbert S. Zim and Lester Ingle

Web Site to Inspire

Steven M. Lewers and Associates Folding Guides, www.foldingguides.com

MORE TO EXPLORE

Now that you have your square assembled, you can take it on the road. Use it together to check out your backyard lawn, a forest floor, or a local pond. Have your child compare and contrast his findings.

TREE HUGGER

Materials

Park or meadow that has a nice variety of trees

A blindfold

A field guide for trees (optional)

Trees offer us so much—they provide shady picnic spots, branches for climbing, and a visual haven to the world. When a child takes the time to hug a tree, she begins to appreciate the often-overlooked trees that we can so easily take for granted. Building these personal connections to the natural world is the first step in helping your child develop a conservation ethic. Be prepared—after this experience your child is likely to ask you to revisit her favorite tree again and again!

This tree-hugger experience will help your child develop a personal connection with the trees in your community. Through this activity your child uses her senses of touch and smell to learn about the characteristics that make each tree distinct.

ONE STEP AHEAD

During the tree-hugger activity your child will explore the various parts of a tree. During the course of his exploration you can help him identify the parts of a tree and the purposes they serve.

Trunk: Helps support the tree's braches and leaves. The trunk is made up of layers, some of which help water and minerals get to the leaves and then carry sap made by the leaves to the branches, trunk, and roots.

Branches: Help transport materials from the trunk to the leaves and from the leaves back down to the roots

Bark: Guards a tree from injuries by providing a protective layer around the trunk

Roots: Grow under the trunk of the tree and help anchor the tree to the ground. They absorb water and minerals from the soil.

Leaves: Collect energy from the sun and convert it into food for the tree

THE PROCESS

Your child will need a partner; it can be you, a sibling, or a friend on a playdate. Start by placing a blindfold on your child. Explain that his partner will guide him to a special tree in the park.

> **Books to Inspire**
>
> *Be a Friend to Trees* by Patricia Lauber
>
> *Tell Me, Tree: All about Trees for Kids* by Gail Gibbons
>
> *The Tree Book for Kids and Their Grown Ups* by Gina Ingoglia
>
> *The Tree in the Ancient Forest* by Carol Reed-Jones
>
> *A Tree Is Nice* by Janice May Udry

Once your child is guided to a tree, encourage him to explore the tree. Suggest that he reach up high, reach down low, feel the ground around the tree, and see if he can find a leaf. Have him hug the tree to feel the texture of its bark, and then describe it (smooth, rough, and so on).[2]

When your child is finished, his partner can walk him back to the center of the park or meadow and then turn him around a couple of times. Now remove the blindfold and ask your child if he can find his tree. As he is searching for his tree, remind him of his earlier discoveries such as how wide the tree felt and what the leaves and bark felt like.

MORE TO EXPLORE

Gather samples of leaves, seeds, and bark, and use a field guide to identify your child's special tree. Come back and visit the tree together throughout the changing seasons. Have your child sketch his observations. During one of your visits you might investigate all the creatures that live in or around your child's special tree.

THE SEASONS OF A TREE

Whether it is the tree your child hugged in the park or a favorite in your own yard, observing a tree as it changes throughout the year is an amazing experience. Monitoring a tree over the course of a year offers children an opportunity to witness and document change over time. Your child will see how a tree's seasonal cycles correspond to other changes in nature that occur throughout the year.

Materials

A blank book or
nature journal

A black fine-point
marker

Drawing pencils

Colored pencils,
watercolor
paints, or oil
pastels

ONE STEP AHEAD

Here are some things that you can encourage your child to look for each
season in and around his favorite tree:

Fall: Leaves changing colors, leaves falling to the ground, the details
and patterns of the branches, insects and other animals living in
the tree

Winter: The tree's shape or silhouette, the bark's texture and colors,
any signs of life, small buds forming on the branches

Spring: Buds starting to grow bigger and then beginning to open,
flowers blooming, the appearance of insects and other animals,
birds or nests

Summer: The shape and details of the new leaves, signs of fruit
growing, evidence of life

THE PROCESS

Have your child choose a favorite tree that she would like to get to know.
Plan at least four visits to the tree (one for each season). The more you
visit the tree, the more your child will notice the subtle nuances and
changes taking place over time.

Have your child pack a small bag that includes her journal and any supplies she would like to use for her observations. As your child records her observations, you can ask her what she notices about the leaves, branches, roots, trunk, bark, and so on.

It is a relaxing and rejuvenating experience—you may want to start your own tree journal!

Books to Inspire

The Ecosystem of an Apple Tree by Elaine Pascoe

The Seasons of Arnold's Apple Tree by Gail Gibbons

Sky Tree: Seeing Science through Art by Thomas Locker

A Tree for All Seasons by Robin Bernard

MORE TO EXPLORE

Aside from sketching the changes your child sees in her tree, there are a number of activities your child can incorporate into her tree journal. Pressing leaves, making bark rubbings, writing poems about her tree, and photographing and labeling the different parts of her tree are wonderful ways to add to your child's understanding and appreciation of trees.

FINISH THE PICTURE: EXPLORATION OF BARK

Materials

A camera

A magnifying glass

Trees in your yard or park

Looking Closely at Bark printable (see page 239)

Being able to differentiate the bark of one tree from another is a skill that comes in handy when trying to identify trees. By looking closely at the bark of a specific tree, children grow beyond the "bark is brown" schema and notice a variety of colors, textures, and patterns.

ONE STEP AHEAD

To explain what bark does, tell your child that it helps to protect a tree from injury, like a knight wearing armor. While your child is engaged in this activity, encourage him to use detailed vocabulary words to describe what he sees. Some words that you can suggest are: smooth, rough, bumpy, hard, soft, thick, thin, light, dark, green, beige, brown, and black.

For this activity a little parental preparation is needed. Start by selecting and photographing the bark on a tree in your yard or a local park. Print the photo so that it is centered on the page (see "Looking Closely at Bark" in "Printables" as a reference).

THE PROCESS

Invite your child to solve a mystery. Let him know that you took a picture of the bark of a tree in your yard (or park) and that you were hoping he could figure out what tree it belongs to. Tell him to study the bark in the photo closely first (a magnifying glass may help). Then have him finish the picture of the tree's trunk based on the details he notices from the photo of the bark. Encourage him to incorporate as many details as possible into his drawing.

After he has completed his picture, take him into the yard (or park) and ask him if he can find the tree that matches his sketch. As your

Books to Inspire

Bark by Catherine Chambers

Trees, Leaves, and Bark by Diane L. Burns

child is searching for a match, encourage him to touch each tree and use words to describe what he feels.

An alternative to this experience is to have your child take a photo of his favorite tree's bark. Print it on a piece of paper and have him finish the picture with a drawing of the whole tree. Whichever approach you choose, it is delightful to see how a child's view of bark opens up as he notices the minutiae and appreciates what makes each tree unique.

MORE TO EXPLORE

Another way to capture the essence of bark is by doing bark rubbings. When you tape or hold a piece of white paper up to a tree's bark and then rub a crayon (on the long side, with the paper peeled) over the paper, your child will pick up the bark's beautiful texture.

NOTICING THE DETAILS: MAKING WIRE LEAVES

During a trip to observe the schools of Reggio Emilia, Italy, I had the opportunity to see this project done with butterflies as the subject. After

doing some research, I discovered Ann Pelo's book *The Language of Art,* where she suggests using wire to make leaves.

When making wire leaves, your child can articulate what she observes about leaves through an interesting artistic medium. This activity encourages children to observe closely, introduces them to scientific vocabulary, and helps to develop their fine motor skills.

If your child has never worked with wire before you may want to give her some time get to know the material before starting this activity. After making wire leaves with the girls, we decided to leave the wire out in our atelier so they could use it to make other sculptures when the mood struck.

Materials

Leaves from your child's favorite tree	Drawing paper
A magnifying glass	A black fine-point pen
A variety of wire (14 to 20 gauge is best for smaller hands), cut into different sizes (available at hardware stores)	Clear fishing line
	Leaf Veins printable (see page 240)

ONE STEP AHEAD

While looking closely at leaves, your child is likely to notice the veins. Be prepared to tell her what veins do. The veins help provide structural support for the leaf. They also bring in water and minerals from the roots and transport the sap that leaves make (through photosynthesis) to various parts of the tree. The pattern of veins on a leaf is referred to as *venation.* While each tree and plant has unique vein patterns, they generally fall into three categories: pinnate, palmate, and parallel (see "Leaf Veins" in "Printables").

THE PROCESS

Start by having your child collect a leaf from her favorite tree. Encourage her to study the leaf with a magnifying glass and ask her what she sees.

When she mentions the veins, ask her to trace the veins with her finger. Now take out the Leaf Veins printable and ask your child if she can recognize which pattern the veins on her leaf has.

It is helpful to have your child do an observational drawing of her leaf before venturing into creating a wire sculpture. We like to use fine-point black markers so the focus is on the details of the leaves' shapes and veins, rather than on the colors. While your child is drawing, suggest that she notice the shape of the leaf, the edges (leaf margin), and the veins.

Once the detailed drawing is complete, your child is ready to create with wire. Start her off with one long piece of wire so she can form the shape of her leaf. She can use her drawing as a guide. Next suggest that she focus on the veins. If needed, you can demonstrate how to join two wire ends by wrapping them together.

When the leaves are complete, you can proudly display them by hanging them with clear fishing line.

Books to Inspire

The Language of Art by Ann Pelo

Leaves in Myth, Magic and Medicine by Alice Thoms Vitale

Trees: North American Trees Identified by Leaf, Bark and Seed by Steven M. L. Aronson

MORE TO EXPLORE

Another fun way to document the veins on a leaf is by doing a leaf rubbing (see "More to Explore" for "Finish the Picture: Exploration of Bark").

5 Exploration of Art and Artists

Every child is an artist. The problem is how to remain an artist once we grow up.

— Picasso

Making and appreciating art is one of life's most fulfilling pleasures. If young children have access to quality materials and are able to participate in a variety of meaningful experiences, they can maintain their uninhibited approach to art for their entire lives. Being part of a child's artistic process is awe-inspiring, and there are many things you can do to nurture your child's ability to express himself through his art and to develop an admiration for the art of others.

Looking at Art with Children

Observing and discussing art with children is both enjoyable and educational. Whether you have access to a museum or simply check out books from the library, exposing your child to great art and artists encourages him to see the world through different eyes. Spending time together, looking at art, and talking about what you both see can open up a world of new techniques and a vocabulary for your child that will enrich his own creative processes. While sharing the art that you most admire with your child is a wonderful experience, discovering his tastes and preferences is a true delight!

In Howard Gardner's essay *Art Education and Human Development*, he offers insight into how children at different stages of development view art. During the younger years children are most attracted to the items within a piece of art that they recognize from their everyday lives. They will often respond enthusiastically to a favorite color, object, or person that reminds them of someone or something special to them. After children have more experience looking at art, they begin to develop preferences for certain artists or styles.[1] You may find that your child gravitates toward a particular artist. My oldest daughter loves Matisse's work and compares every new piece of art we see to his work. During this stage it is helpful to ask your child open-ended questions while looking at art together, such as:

- What do you notice about this painting?
- What is happening in this painting (sculpture, and so on)?
- What colors do you see?
- What objects do you see?
- Do the people in this painting remind you of anyone you know?
- What do you like about this painting?

As children grow a bit older they begin to respond emotionally to the art they encounter. During this stage it is fun to delve more deeply into the specific styles of artists and to speculate about why they made certain choices in their work. Older children can also connect art with certain periods of history. Researching the time period during which a particular piece of art was created and looking for historical references within it can be an interesting endeavor for children in this stage.[2] Children who have consistently created their own art and developed their own personal standards will soon apply them to other people's work. Drawing your child into conversations about which artists remind him of his own work can help him gain new insights into a particular artist as well as his own artistic process.

Some ways to engage your child in this stage while observing art are by asking:

- What feeling do you get when you look at this piece of art?
- How do you think the people in this painting feel?
- Can you see evidence of a particular technique that this artist used?
- What message is the artist trying to convey? How do they convey it?
- Does this piece of art remind you of something from your own life?

Regardless of your child's learning stage, sharing an enthusiasm and appreciation for art is a wonderful way for families to connect. As your children grow, the conversations will take on new meaning, and the possibilities for connections—both personal and academic—are endless.

Talking to Children about Their Art

Although at first glance a child's piece of art may appear to consist of simple lines or scribbles, rest assured that behind the simple marks lies a world of intentions. The way that we talk to our children about their work can either inspire or inhibit their process. For example, when you ask your child, "What are you drawing?" you are implying that you cannot decipher what it is that she has been working so hard to create. When you ask your child, "Can you tell me about your drawing?" you are conveying the message that you would like to know more about her work, and even though you may not know what it is, you are not communicating that to your child. Try asking your child both questions, and you will quickly discover that you get a much more enthusiastic response from the latter one. You can then use her response to generate more specific questions. If your child answers, "It is a picture of the zoo," you can respond by asking, "What animals are at the zoo?" or "What else is at your zoo?"

Asking about and commenting on specific aspects of your child's work encourages her to elaborate more on her thought process. When a child becomes more aware of her own process she can begin to build on it with each new piece of art. The developmental overview that follows presents more suggestions for questions that will help your child talk freely about her work, helping her to explicitly identify and act upon her thinking.

Developmental Overview

Understanding your child's artistic development will give you a window into his thinking process and shed some light on the milestones he will experience along the way. The following developmental stages are based on my own observations of children's art throughout the years and on the work of Nancy Smith in her book *Experience and Art*. Please keep in mind that a child's development may vary from the stages mentioned here, depending on the material he is using. For example, he may have more control using pencils than he has while painting.

Stage I

For very young children, the paintbrush, pen, or pencil they are using becomes a direct extension of their arm. Children during this stage of development learn about the material they are using through repetitive use. This is evident in paintings done by very young children, which often contain the same brushstroke over and over again. At times your child may be so enthusiastic about the effects of his movements that he wears a hole through the paper he is working with. These repetitive movements may appear random at first, but they become more controlled with experience. After a while shapes that may have been formed through accidental movements will appear with clearer intention.[3] Although it may appear that children are simply making a mess, these early art experiences help create a foundation for later artistic expression. Young painters during this stage will also learn through experience that paints change colors when mixed together. Introducing your child to a consistent painting routine (see "Open-Ended Art Explorations") at this stage helps foster independence and makes for smooth transitions for everything from setting up to cleaning up.

During Stage I it is useful to offer feedback to your child that directly pertains to his work. Saying, "What a beautiful picture!" does not give him *specific* feedback on his work. Being specific with your child about what he did and asking him relevant questions help him to become conscious of the effort he made and the results that came from his work.

Here are some possible questions to ask Stage I artists about their work:

- Can you tell me about your picture?
- How did you make that line with your brush (pencil, pen)?
- You used a lot of lines; are they thick or thin?
- What colors did you use together to make that light purple?

Stage II

As children gain more experience with art materials, they can predict how the motions of their hands will translate into recognizable marks on their work. Their marks begin to be clearly separate and intentional, and they start to occupy different spaces on the paper.[4] Remembering to wash her brushes between colors (part of your child's painting routine) will lead to

more control over the shades of the colors in her work. Now that your child is becoming more aware of the power she has to create with a variety of art materials, you can broaden her horizons by offering a variety of tools. "Would you like a long or short piece of paper?" "Would you like a brush that creates thick lines or thin lines?" While your child is at work creating, you can introduce new vocabulary in your questions, such as, "How many ways can you make lines? Wavy? Bumpy? Smooth? Curved? Straight? Thick? Thin? Long? Short?"

Here are some more possible questions to ask Stage II artists about their work:

- Can you tell me about your picture?
- How many lines did you paint?
- Did you start your lines at the top or bottom of the paper?
- Which colors did you use to make the wavy lines? How about the straight lines?

Stage III

"Fire"

During Stage III, children evolve their ability to create specific shapes and forms into making lifelike pictures of their experiences. Your child's images usually will take form as a combination of circles, triangles, rectangles, and other shapes that he has previously mastered. For example, a car may appear as an oval with two circles attached.[5] Early in this stage children will often draw a single object in the middle of a blank page. As your child progresses, he will add related images, such as a road to a picture of a car. It is an exciting time and a delight to witness your child's first representational drawings emerge (definite keepers for the portfolio)! Ask your Stage II artist questions that encourage him to expand upon his ideas and add more details to his work.

Here are some possible questions to ask Stage III artists about their work:

- Can you tell me about your picture?
- You used short, thick lines right here. Did you use any other kinds of lines?
- What shapes did you use to make the flames?
- Where did you see the fire? How did it make you feel?
- Are you going to put yourself in the picture?

Stage IV

At this stage, children's art begins to show dramatic differences, including much greater detail. People are now depicted from different points of view and with more distinguishable body parts and color. Children will often utilize an entire sheet of paper, creating scenes where every object is related to the whole.[6] The topics of your child's art will broaden as she represents a wider array of personal experiences. It is during this stage that your child's drawings become an important aspect of communicating and sharing her ideas with others. With writing skills emerging simultaneously, children will often use drawings to convey meaning in their written stories.

Here are some possible questions to ask Stage IV artists about their work:

- Can you tell me about your picture?
- You used a triangle to make your mom's dress and rectangles to make your dad's pants. What shape did you use to make your body?

- I see that you drew a garden. Is that our garden? What else can we find in our garden?
- I see that you drew a table with food. What is your favorite food on the table?

Now that you are well versed in how your child develops artistically and equipped with some guiding questions that can deepen his experience, the following learning experiences will help to strengthen your child's ability to engage in and appreciate art. Making art together is a lovely way to spend time as a family, so go ahead and indulge in your own creations along with your child. Your enthusiasm will be contagious!

OPEN-ENDED ART EXPLORATIONS

"This is my heart when
I listen to music"

After reviewing the art activities that I included in this chapter, I realized that I had left out a fundamental experience: open-ended art exploration. So, although this section does not include a specific project, I felt that it was necessary to include here as a basis for success in the other art activities. It is essential to provide children with time for self-directed explorations, when they can experiment with art materials and tools, as well as freely express themselves, without any specific guidance from an adult.

As I look back at my daughters' artwork from over the years, it is the pieces they created of their own accord that I treasure most—for they are the pieces that provide glimpses into my girls' personal styles and thoughts.

Materials

Large pieces of paper (plain and water-color)

A variety of paints (such as watercolor and tempera)

A variety of different-sized brushes

Oil pastels

Pens

Colored pencils

Paper and cloth scraps for collage

A small bowl of water and sponge (for watercolors)

Any other art supplies you think your child might enjoy

ONE STEP AHEAD

It is helpful to decide ahead of time what type of routine you would like
to establish with your child in terms of setting up, using, and cleaning
up materials. Consistency sets the stage for successful experiences and
steers children toward independence as they get older.

THE PROCESS

These experiences can start with a request by your child (when she sits in
her Playful Learning space, supplied with creative materials) or following
your suggestion (to paint, draw, play with clay, make a collage, and so on).
When your child is young, you will need to set things up for her, modeling how to take out the art materials and how to put them away. It helps
to store the supplies in well-organized baskets or containers, so your
child will eventually be able to do it for herself. Once she becomes familiar with the routine, she will know how to access the materials whenever
the inspiration hits her.

When your child is ready, you might turn on some soft music or nature
sounds as background music to create a relaxed and peaceful mood.

Make yourself a cup of your favorite tea and quietly sit in on your child's art experience. Be careful not to intervene or direct the activity. Act as a facilitator to the process. Listen to your child describe her endeavors, occasionally asking questions (see the developmental overview for ideas), and jot down a few of her quotes while she's in action. Just writing down one of her comments on the back of a painting or work can shed light on her process years later when you revisit her work.

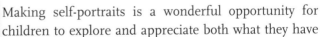

Books to Inspire

The Dot by Peter H. Reynolds

Hands: Growing Up to Be an Artist by Lois Ehlert

How to Paint the Portrait of a Bird by Jacques Prévert

I Am an Artist by Pat Lowery Collins

Ish by Peter H. Reynolds

MORE TO EXPLORE

Over time you can expand your child's open-ended art experiences to include modeling with beeswax, painting with various types of paints, working with clay, oil pastels, charcoal pencils, and more.

SELF-PORTRAITS

Making self-portraits is a wonderful opportunity for children to explore and appreciate both what they have in common with all living beings and what makes them unique. This activity helps your child develop fine motor skills while observing and drawing the intricate details of his own face. Taking the time to look closely, notice the fine points, and record what he sees is a skill that will serve your child well in many areas of his development.

Materials

A large piece of blank paper

Red, yellow, blue, white, and black paint

Paintbrushes in various sizes

Small handheld mirrors

A fine-tip permanent marker

A muffin tin for holding and mixing paints

ONE STEP AHEAD

Before introducing your child to this experience, do a bit of research on self-portraits and find some of your favorites to share with your child. Some child-friendly self-portraits that can easily be found via a quick trip to the library or by doing an image search on the Internet are those by Pablo Picasso, Frida Kahlo, Leonardo da Vinci, and Mary Cassatt.

Another wonderful way to launch an exploration of self-portraits is by reading *The Colors of Us* by Karen Katz. It is a story about a mother and daughter who explore the wonderful nuances of people's skin color. *The Colors of Us* takes us out of a black-and-white world and into a celebration of the multiplicity of skin tones. After reading the book, you can propose that your child create portraits just like the main character of the story.

THE PROCESS

Start by talking about self-portraits. Explain that self-portraits are depictions of an artist created by the artist herself. Showing your child examples of self-portraits by other children or artists will inspire her and reassure her that self-portraits don't have to be exact replicas.

Give your child a small mirror and ask her to look at her face, paying close attention to the details of her eyes, nose, lips, and the shape of her face. A good warm-up activity is to have your child look closely at one part of her face and do a sketch, paying particular attention to lines and the details of what she sees. We started with the mouth (open), and then moved on to the eye.

When your child seems comfortable with the idea of a self-portrait, give her a large fresh sheet of paper so she can work on her face as a whole. Have her use a fine-tip permanent marker to make a black line drawing of her face. Encourage her to continue looking in the mirror. paying close attention to details she observes.

> **Books to Inspire**
>
> *The Colors of Us* by Karen Katz
>
> *Five Hundred Self-Portraits* with introduction by Julian Bell (parental discretion advised)
>
> *Just Like Me: Stories and Self-Portraits by Fourteen Artists* edited by Harriet Rohmer
>
> *Mobility of Expression* by Municipality of Reggio Emilia Infant-Toddler Centers and Preschools

When the drawing is complete, it is time to take on the task of mixing paints to match the color of your child's skin. We started by putting red, blue, yellow, white, and black paints into separate sections of a muffin tin. We used brushes to mix paints together, using a different section for each color we made. To make a brown skin color, start by mixing yellow with a touch of blue to make green. Next add red and then yellow until the brown color comes close to matching your child's shade of skin. If you need a darker brown paint you can add black; if you need a lighter brown tone you can add white. Then move on to creating the other colors that your child would like to include in her portrait. Once her chosen colors have been created, the final step is for her to paint in the remaining details of her black line drawings.

MORE TO EXPLORE

A wonderful tradition is to have your child make a new self-portrait every year. Save all of her yearly self-portraits in the same place so you can see and discuss the changes that occur over the years.

OBSERVATIONAL DRAWINGS

Observational drawing, which relies on close observation, fosters a deeper understanding of a given object. This process encourages your child to slow down and look more closely at everyday objects in order to witness details he wouldn't ordinarily notice.

Materials

A sketchbook or paper

A fine-tip black marker (permanent if you plan to watercolor over
the drawing) or drawing pencils

Watercolor paints, oil pastels, colored pencils (optional)

ONE STEP AHEAD

The best piece of advice that I have found to offer children before they get
started on an observational drawing is that they should notice and follow
the lines that they see within and around the object that they are drawing.
Reading one of the books listed in "Books to Inspire" can set the stage for
noticing and following lines in artwork.

THE PROCESS

Making observational drawings is a wonderful way to encourage children to take in the world around them. A great first choice is to make
an observational drawing of a simple flower in a vase. You can explain to

Books to Inspire

Drawing with Children: A Creative Teaching and Learning Method That Works for Adults Too by Mona Brookes

Follow the Line series by Laura Ljungkvist

Keeping A Nature Journal: Discover a Whole New Way of Seeing the World around You by Clare Walker Leslie and Charles E. Roth

Lines by Philip Yenawine

Lines That Wiggle by Candace Whitman

The Neat Line: Scribbling through Mother Goose by Pamela Duncan Edwards

your child that he is going to do what artists do, which is to look closely, observe, and then create. You can use one of the leaves on the flower as an example and explain that, normally, he might just draw the leaf as a green oval shape. But when he slows down to do an observational drawing, he can really zoom in and notice all of the details. When he looks closely at a leaf, he can see a beautiful pattern with lines that he might not have seen before. Explain (as you do a sketch first) that you are going to make sure that you include every line you see in your drawing.

Invite your child to follow the lines he sees within and around the flower. Then sit quietly and watch his process unfold.

Once your child feels comfortable with the idea of doing observational drawings, he can make them often for both art- and science-based activities. Now both of our daughters have a notebook that they grab when they want to document something that catches their interest. They also enjoy adding watercolors to their sketches to bring them to life.

MORE TO EXPLORE

Observational drawings can be done with a variety of mediums. It is great to start with black ink drawings, because the pen has a smooth, consistent feel for the developing artist. Using drawing pencils and incorporating paints and oil pastels will add a fun, new dimension to your child's work.

JACKSON POLLOCK: ENGAGING IN ABSTRACT ART

In *Storybook Art,* Maryann F. Kohl and Jean Potter recommend using *Olivia* as an entry point for teaching children about Jackson Pollock's art. *Olivia* by Ian Falconer has a scene where the main character (Olivia) does a painting in her house, Jackson Pollock style—and gets in big trouble. Reading *Olivia* together and then having your child undertake an abstract project of her own will help her make a connection between a favorite family read-aloud and a real-world artist—Jackson Pollock. Your child will be thrilled by the notion of freely splattering paint about *without* getting into trouble!

Materials

A blank canvas or large sheet of paper

Blue, red, yellow, and white washable paints

A muffin tin for holding and mixing paints

Paintbrushes

A bucket of water

A tarp

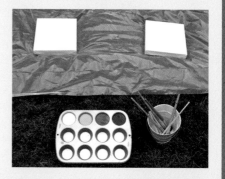

ONE STEP AHEAD

Gathering books and videos about Jackson Pollock and his work before undertaking this experience will deepen your child's connection to the artist behind the technique as well as inspire enthusiasm about trying out Pollock's techniques.

THE PROCESS

After reading *Olivia* by Ian Falconer, you can mention to your child that there was an artist who painted the same way that Olivia did in the story. It is helpful to have a bit of information on Jackson Pollock handy. I picked up a couple of books at the library so we could look at his art and explore the techniques that he used. My girls were captivated by the fact that he preferred to paint with his canvas on the floor.

If your child is inspired to start creating abstract art, take her outside to begin her masterpiece. Set up a large plastic tarp to cover the area your child will be painting on. Start out by giving her the primary colors and white washable tempera paint. Encourage your child to mix the colors in a muffin tin that she would like to use in her painting. This is a great opportunity to introduce or review the basics of color mixing.

Once your child's palette is complete, give her a blank canvas, some brushes, and let her drip away!

Books to Inspire

Action Jackson by Jan Greenberg and Sandra Jordan

The Life and Work of . . . Jackson Pollock by Leonie Bennett

Olivia by Ian Falconer

Pollock by Elizabeth Frank

Storybook Art by Maryann F. Kohl and Jean Potter

MORE TO EXPLORE

Now that your child has been introduced to abstract art, expand on her experience by researching and learning about the techniques and art of other abstract artists such as Pablo Picasso and Paul Klee.

GEORGIA O'KEEFFE: NATURE IN ART

Learning about the life and work of a particular artist is a great introduction to biographies. As we ventured down the road of studying art and artists, my girls felt personal connections with both the beautiful pieces of work they were discovering and the person behind the art. Georgia O'Keeffe's larger-than-life portrayals of flowers present everyday things to children with a fresh perspective.

ONE STEP AHEAD

If you feel enthusiastic about a piece of art, your child will pick up on it. Spend some time at your local library looking through images of Georgia O'Keeffe's work, and select several books with some of your favorite pieces. Identify a few specific things that you like about each one so you can share them with your child.

Materials

A large canvas or sheet of paper

Watercolor paints

An easel or hard surface (to bring outside to support the paper or canvas)

A variety of different sized paintbrushes

THE PROCESS

Choose an aspect of Georgia O'Keeffe's work that speaks to your child personally. My daughters became fascinated with the *bigness* of her work.

Create an opportunity for your child to experiment with her preferred O'Keeffe technique. One beautiful summer afternoon the girls decided to choose a flower in the garden and bring it to life à la Georgia O'Keeffe. You might set out some images that reflect the style that inspires your child. I put out some books with images of O'Keeffe's large flowers to remind the girls to go big with their own images. It was interesting to watch their process. Although they loved the largeness of O'Keeffe's work, they started small and then gradually grew their flowers from the center out.

As your child continues to work on her creation, point out different things that you notice about both your child's and O'Keeffe's work. For the girls, I pointed out the way that O'Keeffe combined her watercolors. She blended her oranges, yellows, and reds within a single flower, adding a deeper dimension to her paintings. As the girls' flowers grew in size so did their sense of accomplishment. There seemed to be something liberating about filling a canvas with one large flower.

Books to Inspire

Georgia O'Keeffe by Mike Venezia

Georgia O'Keeffe: American and Modern by Charles C. Eldredge

Georgia O'Keeffe: Portraits of Women Artists for Children by Robyn Montana Turner

Georgia Rises: A Day in the Life of Georgia O'Keeffe by Kathryn Lasky

My Name Is Georgia by Jeanette Winter

Through Georgia's Eyes by Rachel Rodriguez

MORE TO EXPLORE

Invite your child to create other pieces of art that reflect the same *bigness* as O'Keeffe's flowers by having her focus on an object in nature of her choosing and then painting a picture of it—filling up a whole canvas or sheet of paper with all of the details and colors she sees.

Materials

A photo or picture from a magazine (preferably of a nature scene)

9 x 12 inch canvas or sheet of paper

Small brushes

Mod Podge (matte)

A variety of acrylic paints

A muffin tin for holding and mixing paints

ONE STEP AHEAD

The Magical Garden of Claude Monet by Laurence Anholt is a great resource for introducing your child to the life and work of Claude Monet, a great impressionist painter. Plan a family walk or outing during sunset at a favorite outdoor location. Bring your camera and encourage your child to take a few photographs of the lovely scene. Little will your child know that her photograph will be used to create a beautiful piece of impressionist art!

THE PROCESS

Have your child select a photograph that she took on your outing or a picture of a nature scene from a magazine. Invite her to use a brush to paint Mod Podge on the back of her photo and then attach it to a canvas. Next have her apply a thin coat of Mod Podge over the top of her photo and the entire canvas.

While letting your child's photo dry completely, you can talk to her about Monet's work, which is referred to as impressionism. Impressionist painters are known for combining a lot of small brushstrokes to make their pictures.

Look closely at some pictures of Monet's paintings together and then ask your child if she can identify the small brushstrokes. Some of Monet's paintings that are particularly helpful for this are *Haystacks*, *The Water-Lily Pond*, and *Sunrise*, and they are easily found online or in your local library.

When the Mod Podge is dry, invite your child to paint over her photograph using small brushstrokes like Monet's.[7] If your child's photograph does not cover her entire canvas, suggest that she continue painting brushstrokes to the edge of her painting.

Books to Inspire

A Blue Butterfly: A Story about Claude Monet by Bijou Le Tord

Claude Monet: Sunshine and Waterlilies by Steven Packard

The Magical Garden of Claude Monet by Laurence Anholt

Monet and the Impressionists for Kids by Carol Sabbeth

MORE TO EXPLORE

Expand your child's impressionist art practice by exploring the lives and art of other impressionist painters, such as Pierre-Auguste Renoir or Mary Cassatt.

6   Growing Globally

New and broader global visions are needed to prepare children and youth to be informed, engaged and critical citizens in the new millennium.
                                                    —Marcelo M. Suárez-Orozco

Our world is growing more and more interconnected every day. All one has to do is trace the origins of the food on the dinner table to realize that we are all part of an interdependent global community where peoples' actions in one region can have enormous impacts on another. Our children are more likely to learn, live, interact, and work with a wider array of people from different religious, linguistic, racial, national, and philosophical backgrounds than any other generation before them.[1] With this reality comes the need for all children to grow up with an understanding and appreciation for the world around them.

A solid knowledge of geography is essential in developing a global awareness. Learning the names and boundaries of each country, however, is not enough to prepare your child for life in the twenty-first century. It is equally important to nurture an understanding of and appreciation for the cultures, history, traditions, and belief systems of the people who reside within those boundaries. As your child develops his social and emotional skills, he will need to develop worldly sensibilities as well to help him navigate our diverse and ever-changing world. This chapter and the next will provide you with ideas and opportunities for exploring the world with your child and discovering all it has to offer.

Developmental Overview

Stage I

Young children love to learn about the world. There is something about getting to know the ways of people in far-off places that both intrigues young children and comforts them. As your child realizes he is part of a much larger global community, he will feel connected to something bigger than himself.

I recommend having a world map accessible to even your youngest child so he will become accustomed to and excited about finding and identifying people and places that pique his interest. While children in Stage I may not retain all the information they are taking in about different parts of the world, the exposure at a young age instills an enthusiasm and desire for exploration that will last through their lives.

For Stage I geographers, finding places on the map with which they have a personal connection, such as places that friends and loved ones are from or have visited, is a wonderful adventure. Often children will overhear the names of different states or countries, but do not have a context for understanding what or where they are. Once your child has made a connection between names and places, he will enjoy learning about the flags, foods, and traditions of the region that interests him.

Though children in Stage I enjoy learning about different parts of the world, their mapping skills are firmly planted in their immediate environment. The best way to introduce your young child to making maps is to begin with his room, your home, and your backyard. Starting with familiar territory helps him take the abstract leap into making and reading maps. During Stage I children are more successful when they can *build* replicas of their favorite places. Research shows that young children who use three-dimensional objects to build models create maps that are more accurate than those who draw them with pen and paper.[2] Wooden unit blocks are a great resource for young geographers to demonstrate their understanding of the places they encounter. When left out for easy access, your child will often use his blocks to re-create scenes from recent experiences. The structures he builds will help strengthen his spatial abilities too. Playing board games also helps children strengthen their awareness of space and their ability to locate places on a map.

Stage II

Once children have mastered their immediate surroundings, they are ready to explore new territories such as their neighborhood, city, and state. Just as your child's daily life is opening up to include people and places outside of the home, so is her ability and interest in mapping larger terrains.[3] It is a time of transition as your child moves from building maps to drawing maps. Your child's newfound ability to make representational drawings allows her to draw more accurate and detailed depictions of the world around her. Children are natural mapmakers, and it is a delight to witness the abundance and diversity of maps your child can come up with when her writing skills catch up to her ideas.

Using well-known streets as material for making maps and coordinating local scavenger hunts is a fun and concrete orientation for Stage II geographers to use while expanding their skills. As you are exploring your neighborhood together, you can introduce your child to geographic concepts, such as the compass rose, cardinal directions, scale, and using map grids to locate places on local maps. These skills, learned within the context of your child's own town, will serve her well as she goes on to explore more complex types of maps. It is handy to have a variety of maps around the house to serve as references as your child begins to explore surrounding areas.

Stage III

Once children have grounded themselves in their own personal places, they are able to solidify their understanding of where they are on a map. At this point your child has developed an internal compass with her home and community as a reference point, which makes it possible to expand her perspective to include the world at large. She has already had a lot of positive experiences using a variety of maps and is starting to make connections between new information and the areas of the world she has already explored.

During this stage you will see how the pieces of the puzzle come together for your child as she moves back and forth from the local to the global in the maps she creates. Abstract concepts, such as continents and countries, become more tangible as the ability to connect different people and cultures to specific places on a map matures. This is a wonderful time to fully utilize your world map, adding markers to places your family has discussed, read about, or traveled to. The markers serve as a way to organize and cross-reference bits of information you glean together about different countries around the world.

Children are always taking in information about the world around them. At school your child may be learning about your city and state, while hearing about our country and many other places at home. Therefore it is difficult for her to learn about geography in any sort of linear progression. By taking your child through the experiences in this chapter, you will help her to develop a greater global awareness. As your child progresses from mapping her room to mapping the world, these foundational activities will provide a reference as she assimilates more and more data about the world.

Building a Multicultural Library

A great place to start in helping your child develop a global perspective is through exposure to a variety of children's books that offer multiple views of the world. Infuse your family reading time with books that offer your child a glimpse into people and places all over the world. Discuss things that all humans share, such as love for family, the need for homes, learning, and working. Talk about the things that are different among cultures, such as the types of homes we live in, the food we eat, and the holidays we celebrate. Encourage your child to write notes about things that stand out to him, and then add them to an interactive world map (which we'll create later). Leave out a collection of books about different places so your child can browse through them on his own.

See page 262 of the resource section for a list of our most beloved multicultural books. Add books you have never read before to your must-checkout library list, and collect your favorite titles for your home library.

Note: Many of the books I recommend showcase lifestyles and cultures from around the world. Some of the images may seem "different" to your child, as they depict ways of life that are unfamiliar to her. As a family, we found that it was helpful to share the "Do You Need It or Do You Want It?" experience, in the next chapter, before diving into many of these books. By having a clear idea of what a want is versus a need, the girls were able to have more meaningful conversations about what they noticed in many of the books we explored.

Web Site to Inspire

The Crafty Crow: A Children's Craft Collective, http://belladia
.typepad.com/crafty_crow/crafts-around-the-world

EXPLORING MY ROOM

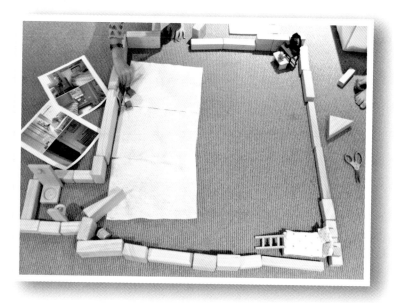

Start your child's mapmaking adventures by having him re-create a space he is familiar with. Constructing a three-dimensional model of his own room introduces your child to the concept of scale and strengthens his ability to recognize and represent spatial relationships.

ONE STEP AHEAD

Your child's first mapmaking and map reading experiences can be challenging, as he is just beginning to develop his spatial awareness. Don't expect exact representations from your child's first models. Rather than correcting mistakes, encourage your child to go stand by or touch the areas in his room he may have misrepresented. As with all the learning experiences in this book, keep it fun and lighthearted, remembering that each activity is a building block that serves as a strong foundation for your child.

Materials

Wooden blocks or other materials for building

Pictures from magazines or catalogs

Fabric scraps

Any other small objects that can represent different parts of your child's room

Books to Inspire

Me on the Map by
    Joan Sweeney

My Map Book by
    Sara Fanelli

THE PROCESS

My Map Book by Sara Fanelli is a great book to read together before doing this activity. As you look through all the different types of maps in the book, spend some time discussing the "Map of My Bedroom." (If you don't wish to buy it, this book is available in public libraries.) When you have finished reading, invite your child to make a map of his room.

Spend some time together in his room looking everything over, and then brainstorm some ideas for materials he could use to represent different things. If possible, have your child build the model in his room, so he can continually check his work. If it is not convenient, then have your child take pictures of the different areas in his room and use them as guides while he is building elsewhere.

Watch your child go to work. You will learn a lot about your child's spatial awareness. Observe the proceedings, and jump in only when needed to help solve a problem that is inhibiting the process.

When your child is finished, encourage him to take a picture of his finished model—before the deconstruction takes place.

MORE TO EXPLORE

Leave your child's building materials in an accessible place and encourage him to build models of other rooms in your home or of places you have been together. For example, if you go to the zoo you can build a replica together when you get home and it is still fresh in your minds.

MAPPING MY HOUSE: A TREASURE HUNT

Children love to make maps that serve a specific purpose. Preparing a treasure hunt for a sibling or friend is the perfect motivation for your child to create her first two-dimensional map. This experience gives your child the opportunity to create, interpret, and then use maps.

Materials

A large piece of paper

Black and red fine-point pens

Pennies for hiding

ONE STEP AHEAD

Besides offering the inspiration, there is not much you need to do to prepare for this experience. Sit back and watch your child's enthusiasm and mapping skills flourish!

THE PROCESS

Build on your child's interest in mapmaking by proposing that she create a treasure map. Explain that you have three pennies (treasures) for her to hide anywhere in the house, and you (or a sibling or friend) will use the treasure map she makes to find them.

Have your child make a map of the house first with a black fine-point marker. If you are doing this activity with two children, encourage both of them to make a map so they can switch and find each other's treasures. As your child is drawing, discuss different parts of your home as she incorporates them into her map. It is interesting to note which parts of the house your child includes first and where the greatest emphasis is placed.

When your child's map is complete, invite her to make a red *X* on the map where she would like to hide her pennies. Next, encourage your child to use her map to hide the pennies in the same spot in the house as

Books to Inspire

I Spy Treasure Hunt: A Book of Picture Riddles by Jean Marzollo

Treasure Hunt by Allan Ahlberg

The Treasure Map by Trisha Speed Shaskan

the one denoted by her red X. Then have the players exchange maps (if there is more than one child participating), and enjoy the treasure hunt! If your child wants to repeat the treasure hunt over and over again, have her use different colors for the Xs. Your child may also want to make adaptations to her map as she continues to use it—a welcome endeavor!

MORE TO EXPLORE

Expand your child's treasure hunt mapping to include your backyard. It is also great fun to pack your supplies and take the treasure hunt to the park.

A NEIGHBORHOOD PUZZLE

Creating a neighborhood map allows your child to develop his mapmaking skills within the confines of familiar territory. This activity, a precursor to reading maps, helps children develop their spatial skills and sense of direction.

> **Materials**
>
> A large piece of blank paper
>
> A camera
>
> A glue stick
>
> A black fine-point marker

ONE STEP AHEAD

Choose a street to map that your child has walked up and down in both directions many times. Your child's familiarity with the street you choose will lead to a fun and successful mapping experience.

THE PROCESS

Walk the street you have chosen to map with your child, and invite him to take pictures of his favorite buildings or landmarks. For example, if you are on Main Street, USA, encourage your child to take pictures of every other shop or so. You may want to snap a picture of each location he chooses to ensure that you will have one good snapshot of each place.

When you return home, print and then cut out the photos with your child.

Now reconstruct the street on a large piece of paper, gluing photos onto the paper in the correct locations. It may help for you to draw something like the street or a central component that will give your child a starting point for placing photos. If your child needs a prompt, encourage him to close his eyes and imagine himself walking down the street. What does he see? What comes next?

Save or display the map for future reference.

Books to Inspire

On the Town: A Community Adventure by Judith Caseley

Only One Neighborhood by Marc Harshman and Barbara Garrison

MORE TO EXPLORE

The next learning experience, which introduces map reading, is a great way to build on this exercise.

A NEIGHBORHOOD PUZZLE PART TWO: CAN YOU FIND IT?

A neighborhood scavenger hunt encourages children to read maps using a grid, employs their sense of direction, and develops their spatial awareness. Terms such as compass rose, north, south, east, and west can be introduced as children describe various locations on a map.

Materials

The map your child created for "The Neighborhood Puzzle"

Photos of items from the street you are mapping

A black marker

A clipboard for writing on the go

Can You Find It? printable (see page 241)

ONE STEP AHEAD

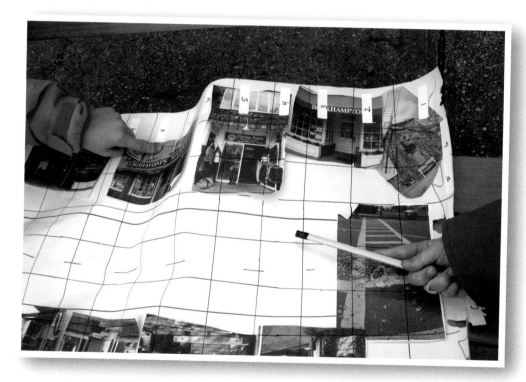

Begin with the map your child made in "The Neighborhood Puzzle." Use a ruler and a black pen to draw a grid over the entire map. Label the rows numerically and the columns alphabetically.

On your own, take photos of little things on the street you are mapping and that are near the landmarks your child photographed. Examples are a recognizable plant, sign, bike rack, and so on. Place the photos in the column labeled "item" on the Can You Find It? printable. In the column labeled "location," write the coordinates from your map where the item is located, such as G15 or A7.

I must admit that during the preparation for this activity, I questioned whether the amount of effort was worth the experience the girls would have. Now that I am on the other end of it, I can assure you that it is worthwhile. The girls turned the corner (no pun intended) in their confidence with directions and their ability to read maps.

THE PROCESS

There are two magical words that inspire enthusiasm within all children—*scavenger* and *hunt*. After telling your children that you have organized a scavenger hunt for them, they will be eager to hear what is to follow. I picked the girls up from school one day with map and clipboards in hand. I explained that I was going to take them on a special adventure, and they would need their map to find some interesting items.

Once you arrive at your street, introduce your child to the grid that you added to his map. Explain that a grid can help him find things on maps. Together, find the coordinates that correlate to a couple of familiar locations on his map.

Next give your child the Can You Find It? sheet that you prepared ahead of time. Explain that he will be able to find the items in the pictures by locating the coordinates on the map and going to that location.

> **Books to Inspire**
>
> *Follow That Map! A First Book of Mapping Skills* by Scot Ritchie
>
> *Treasure Map* by Stuart J. Murphy

After your child has had a couple of successful discoveries with this mapping adventure, his momentum and enthusiasm will take on a life of their own.

MORE TO EXPLORE

Now that your child has had experience using a grid to locate items on a map, introduce him to other local maps and ask him to find familiar places using the coordinates.

FLAGS OF THE WORLD

Learning about the flags of the world is an exciting enterprise for young children. I introduced this activity to my children before the opening ceremonies of the Olympics. The girls loved recognizing and admiring the different flags and have maintained an interest ever since. This experience introduces children to a variety of countries around the world and helps to develop their fine motor skills, word and letter recognition, and pattern identification.

ONE STEP AHEAD

You may want to create the labels for this activity ahead of time, anticipating the countries your child will most likely want to explore first. Once your child gets going with identifying and coloring flags, it is nice to have the labels ready.

THE PROCESS

Start by generating a list with your child of the countries with which you have personal connections. We started out with nine countries that either we had traveled to, knew someone else who had traveled there, or knew someone who was from there.

Next print out or copy small versions of the flags (two of each flag) that you have selected. Invite your child to color in the flags using a Web site or a book as a reference (probably the same resource you used to generate the paper copies).

When the flags are complete, glue them onto small sheets of construction paper for added durability. The last step is to add a label (I printed

Books to Inspire

Complete Flags of the World by Smithsonian Handbooks

Flags of the World by Sylvie Bednar

Flagtastic Flags by Rebecca Howard

ours on return address labels) for each flag. Have your child return to the book or Web site they were using when coloring as a reference for the country names. This step is great for your child as he works to match the letters he sees to the correct flag.

Play games with your child's cards, such as Memory or Go Fish. For younger children, it helps to start with only a few flags and then incorporate more as they master the first set.

WEB SITES TO INSPIRE

Colouring Book of Flags, http://flagspot.net/flags/cbk.html

Central Intelligence Agency, https://www.cia.gov/library/publications/the-world-factbook/docs/flagsoftheworld.html

MORE TO EXPLORE

Have your child continue to add more flags to his collection as he becomes more and more interested in a variety of places around the world.

PIECING IT TOGETHER: THE CONTINENTS

This experience is a great way for your child to solidify her knowledge of the seven continents. By adding your country, state, and home to the map, it allows your child to explore her place in relation to the rest of the world. After starting out with a macro view of the whole world, she will move into a micro view by placing her home on the same map.

Materials

A globe or world map

Tracing paper

A pencil

A hot glue gun

Fabric scissors

Six pieces of blue felt

Ten pieces of different colored felt
(seven for the continents, one for
your country, one for your state, and
one for your house)

White paper cut into small rectangles
for labels

ONE STEP AHEAD

Spending some time reading about the continents and exploring maps together before getting started will go a long way in ensuring a successful mapping experience for your child.

To prepare for this activity, use a hot glue gun to join together the six pieces of blue felt. This large piece of felt will serve as the backdrop for your child's map.

THE PROCESS

After reading about and discussing the continents, spend time with your child exploring the globe and then identify the continents together.

Explain to your child that together you will make a map of the world. Invite her to trace and label each continent, then your country, and then your state (the state will be tiny, but doable) with a pencil and piece of tracing paper. I like to use a globe for this experience, because it illustrates to children how the round world is represented as a flat map.

Ask your child to lay out each piece of tracing paper (continent) on the large piece of blue felt as a review of how the continents will correctly fit on your map.

Next, pin the tracing paper to different colors of felt, and cut out each continent that your child traced. Be sure to cut out a small shape that represents your home to add to the map! While you are cutting, ask your child to write the name of each continent, the country in which you live, and your state on small pieces of white paper. It may help to have a list or book handy that your child can refer to as she writes the names.

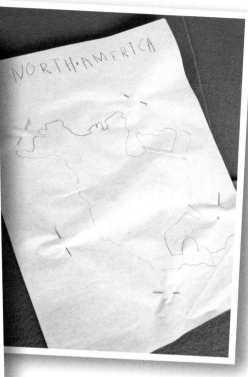

Books to Inspire

Beginner's World Atlas by National
    Geographic

Me on the Map by Joan Sweeney

The Seven Continents by Wil Mara

Where Do I Live? by Neil Chesanow

Lay out the continents on the table and invite your child to assemble the pieces on the large blue background. An atlas is a handy reference for this task.

Once your child has put all the continents in their proper locations, present her with the felt pieces that represent the country and state you live in. Once your country and state are in place, encourage your child to add the finishing piece—your home.

MORE TO EXPLORE

Leave this map puzzle out for your child to play with. Repeated use will benefit your child tremendously as she travels from global explorations to local places and back again.

WHO LIVES HERE?
ADVENTURES IN LONGITUDE AND LATITUDE

Now that your child has been introduced to the idea of using a grid to find places on a map, she is ready to start exploring longitude and latitude lines. With some practice your child will quickly realize that she can locate any place in the world. This experience also reinforces your child's knowledge of the cardinal directions and her ability to identify the continents, countries, and states on a world map.

ONE STEP AHEAD

To prepare for this experience you need to identify the latitude and longitude coordinates for the homes of friends or family with whom your child is familiar. I used Google Earth, which can be downloaded for free (and is rather amazing!); simply type in an address, and you will get the information you need.

Write the information you gather in the first column of the Who Lives Here? printable. To simplify this experience I only asked the girls to find locations using the degrees (°) and omitted the minutes (') and seconds (").

Some helpful terms for this experience include the following:

> *Latitude lines (parallels):* Run across a map, going east and west

> *Equator:* The latitude line in the middle of the earth. It divides the northern and southern hemispheres.

> *Poles:* The North Pole is 90° north, and the South Pole is 90° south

Materials

A map of the world that has latitude and longitude lines

A pencil

Who Lives Here? printable (see page 242)

Longitude lines (meridians): Run up and down a map, going north and south, and meet at the poles

Prime meridian: At 0° longitude, it divides the eastern and western hemispheres

THE PROCESS

Explain to your child that you have a mystery for her to solve. Introduce her to the latitude and longitude lines on your word map, and tell her that the lines can help her find any place in the world using the right coordinates (similar to the grid lines she used in "Neighborhood Puzzle Part Two: Can You Find It?").

Invite your child to identify the coordinates you have provided for some familiar local places. With each location that your child discovers, ask her if she knows who lives there and have her write the name(s) in the second column of the Who Lives Here? printable. After finding and identifying the first couple of locations with you, your child should be able to do the rest independently.

> ### Books to Inspire
>
> *Earth from Above* by Yann Arthus-Bertrand
>
> *Latitude and Longitude* by Rebecca Aberg

MORE TO EXPLORE

Once your child has mastered the idea of locating places on a map by degrees of longitude and latitude, you can introduce her to the finer elements of minutes (') and seconds ("). You can also have your child check her work by entering the addresses of the people you included on your list into Google Earth. The results are dramatic, and your child can watch the program zoom in from a view of the Earth to the specific location she is seeking.

Another fun activity is to look through *Earth from Above* by Yann Arthus-Bertrand—a breathtaking book that showcases aerial photographs of places all over the world. Using the latitude and longitude coordinates provided in the book, have your child locate your family's favorite places on the map.

INTERACTIVE WORLD MAP

Having a world map on display in your home to keep track of the people and places your family cares about helps to consolidate your child's geography skills. Regularly engaging with and keeping track of information on a world map will develop your child's understanding of places around the world on a deeper level. Your child will move beyond simply memorizing names and start to make connections between cultures, languages, traditions, news events, and stories he hears.

ONE STEP AHEAD

To create enthusiasm for this experience, read *Mapping Penny's World* by Loreen Leedy. This book is a great introduction to using keys (or legends) to identify different places on a map.

Materials

A world map

Sticky notes in different colors

A pen or pencil

Map Key printable (see page 243)

A variety of books about the world (see "Building a Multicultural Library" on page 152)

THE PROCESS

To start, choose a few topics for your child to track on a world map. Select a different color sticky note to represent each topic. For example, we chose red to represent "places we know" and yellow to represent "ways to say hello."

Using the Map Key printable, create a legend to correlate with the topics and colors you have selected.

Have your child add new notes to the map as he learns new things and discovers interesting places. Eventually your child will see some overlap and make connections between the people, places, languages, and traditions of the world.

Books to Inspire

Hello World: Greetings in 42 Languages around the Globe! by Manya Stojic

Hottest Coldest Highest Deepest by Steve Jenkins

Mapping Penny's World by Loreen Leedy

Throw Your Tooth on the Roof: Tooth Traditions from around the World by Selby B. Beeler

Wish: Wishing Traditions around the World by Roseanne Thong

MORE TO EXPLORE

Your whole family can add to your child's interactive world map to keep track of places you travel to together, places friends or family travel to, places you receive letters from, and so on. It is also fun to add stickers that represent flags of the world.

For more books with a global emphasis, refer to "Building a Multicultural Library."

7 Raising the Citizens of Tomorrow

Peace cannot be kept by force, it can only be achieved through understanding.
—Albert Einstein

As we move further into the twenty-first century, it is more imperative than ever that parents take an active role in their child's intellectual, emotional, and moral development. A new set of skills and values are becoming critical for success. As we are presently a witness to the rapidly changing economic system, it is easy to see, for example, that the jobs of today will not necessarily be the opportunities of tomorrow. So how can parents best prepare their children for an ever-changing world? "Social and emotional intelligence" has been a catchphrase in the field of education for some years now, but what does it really mean? Is it just more of "that touchy-feely stuff," or could it actually be a significant factor in your child's success?

Current brain research suggests that the area in a child's brain that regulates social and emotional functions, such as managing stress, undergoes major growth until she is in her mid-twenties. The development of a child's neural pathways is hugely dependent on her daily experiences.[1] A child who has been lovingly taught strategies for managing various social situations within a safe environment is better equipped to handle life's challenges than one who has not. As a classroom teacher and a parent, I have witnessed firsthand the enormous benefits that come from explicitly introducing social and emotional skills to children. When children have the necessary language and communication skills to effectively express themselves and to navigate through a variety of circumstances, they have more energy and time to dedicate to playing, learning, and growing.

Through my years of research and teaching in the area of social and emotional learning, I have found myself repeatedly coming back to an organization called CASEL (the Collaborative for Academic, Social, and Emotional Learning—a nonprofit that strives to bring social and emotional learning to all children). CASEL's Web site (www.casel.org) is a tremendous resource for academics, schools, and families. CASEL has identified five essential social and emotional skills that all children should learn. Not only are these competencies critical for the healthy development of our children—they are fundamental to the future of our planet.

Self-awareness: To recognize, understand, and label feelings and to acknowledge and nurture personal capabilities

Social awareness: To understand the perspectives of others and to appreciate that everyone has different points of view and experiences that shape who they are

Self-management: To manage feelings in a positive manner and set productive goals to work toward

Responsible decision making: To evaluate situations and make sound decisions on how to respond; the ability to take personal responsibility by acting in an honest and ethical way, demonstrating respect for others

Relationship skills: To utilize strong communication skills to build positive relationships with others; to be comfortable saying "no" to situations that are not ethical or safe[2]

The learning experiences in this chapter offer parents ideas for starting conversations, developing a shared language of respect, and introducing social and emotional skills to your child that will serve her throughout her lifetime. Exploring these concepts together as a family has been a transformative process for us and has helped us to create a culture of respect in our home. This culture of respect acts as a foundation that guides us—

both as a family and as individuals in our daily lives. It is an incredible joy to witness the thoughtful insights and strategies that young children bring to complex situations when they are given the proper tools and language.

> ### Web Site to Inspire
> The Collaborative for Academic, Social, and Emotional Learning,
>   www.casel.org

Developmental Overview

Stage I

Children's feelings are at the forefront during Stage I of their social and emotional development. Learning to identify feelings and becoming aware of the feelings of others is an objective worth working toward. Research suggests that a child's ability to identify and effectively manage his feelings and emotions not only makes him happier, but also leads to higher academic success. By proactively introducing your child to the vocabulary associated with different feelings in a lighthearted and playful manner, he will be better equipped to communicate with you and deal with his emotions during more "charged" moments.

Parents can play an important role in helping to reflect their children's feelings back to them. This mirroring helps your child feel validated and better understand himself. Simply stating "I see that you are sad because you have to leave your friend's house" can subdue what could be a difficult and awkward situation. It also works well to have a conversation validating your child's feelings before an event that you know may be challenging. "I realize that you may feel sad when it is time to leave your playdate, but we have an appointment this afternoon, and I really need you to be ready to go when I get there." The preface validates your child's feelings and gives him time to deal with his emotions before the actual pickup takes place. Of course, it is also nice to appreciate your child when all goes well. "I really appreciate that you left your playdate without crying today. Now we will be right on time for the doctor."

It is equally important that, as adults, we articulate and deal with our own emotions in a positive manner. I have made an effort to revisit situations in which I may have not been such a great model. "I am sorry for getting angry at you. I felt frustrated when I saw your clothes on the floor because I had just finished doing the laundry. I should not have raised my voice." Over time your child's vocabulary and emotional comfort level will grow as he learns that feelings are a part of everyday life and can be handled in a healthy way.

Books are a wonderful way to introduce new concepts and vocabulary to young children and to stimulate meaningful conversations. Discussing the various characters and how they respond to their emotions can be a very helpful exercise. Some of our favorite books about feelings are:

Feelings by Aliki

Feelings to Share from A to Z by Todd Snow, Peggy Snow, Pamela Espeland, and Carrie Hartman

My Many Colored Days by Dr. Seuss

Quick as a Cricket by Audrey Wood

As children in Stage I begin to move from parallel play (when children play near each other but do not interact) to actively engaging with other children, it is a good idea to start incorporating a language of respect into your daily activities. Too often adults believe that young children are not capable of understanding the effects of their behavior. After years of working with young children, I have observed quite the opposite. Through thoughtful interactions and experiences with friends and loved ones, children quickly internalize the value of and demonstrate respectful behavior. Addressing concepts such as showing respect, sharing, taking turns, naming feelings, and being honest within the context of their daily routines helps children to understand their importance. Although at first your child might not fully grasp the meaning of those terms, repeated discussions during a variety of relevant situations will reinforce the concepts, and soon your child will integrate them into his behavior. Notice out loud when you see another child being respectful or sharing, and discuss the specific behaviors that you observed. Be sure to label disrespectful behavior when it happens in your home too. "Sarah, your sister asked you to stop tickling her, and you did not stop. It is important that you respect her body and her words." When children are raised in an environment where the nuances of respect and disrespect are discussed and explored openly, they quickly become eloquent advocates for themselves, and others.

Stage II

The family is a microcosm of the larger world, and the way relationships are managed at home will set the course for your child's external interactions. Being clear about expectations is very important during this stage. It has helped our family to have a few nonnegotiable rules that we uphold consistently. Our family rules are that we must always have respect for each other's feelings, words, bodies, and things. Keeping our expectations simple and making them explicit from the beginning has helped our daughters learn about respect through numerous family experiences within a safe and loving environment.

As your child's ability to communicate grows, she will become more adept at expressing her feelings and then at generating solutions to conflicts that arise. Continue with the work you have been doing during Stage I, and now expand upon it by giving your child specific techniques to use in resolving disputes or handling other challenges that come her way (see the "ABCs of Conflict Resolution"). Encouraging your child to use her words to identify and express herself during a conflict goes a long way in helping her to come up with a resolution or compromise. Although children in Stage II are learning to devise solutions, they often still need guidance during more emotional moments. Expecting your child to work through conflicts on her own is a good idea in theory, but not very effective until she has been taught specific strategies for doing so. The good news is that children in this stage are eager to learn and use these skills and are very proud when they can solve problems on their own.

Now that your child is well versed in the language of feelings and respect, she is ready to start learning about other social nuances, such as nonverbal communication and how the tone of a person's voice can change the meaning of a person's words. Role-playing different scenarios is a lighthearted way to explore these subtleties. A few phrases that can feel positive if said with a kind tone, yet feel negative if said gruffly, include: "Go ahead," "I'll get it," and "That's fine with me." By saying these phrases to each other and experimenting with how tone changes their meaning, your child will get the idea quickly. The same approach can be used to explore nonverbal communication. You can start by asking, "Is there a way to give a 'put-up' without using words?" "How about a 'put-down'?" Next, you can take turns demonstrating examples of nonverbal "put-ups," such as a smile, and "put-downs," such as turning your back on someone.

Stage III

By the time children reach Stage III their social worlds are in full force. Now is the time when your child will transfer the skills learned at home to a wider circle of friends and acquaintances. During this stage, his newly acquired communication skills will serve both you and your child well. The experiences he has had at home will serve as reference points for new situations and confrontations. Keeping lines of communication open is essential so that your child feels comfortable talking with you about his experiences.

I have found that during this stage the quantity of time spent with children becomes a determining factor in their willingness to open up. It always seems that my daughter's story about the girl who did not want to play with her surfaces (out of the blue) at the end of a long afternoon spent together. These stories most certainly do not come up with the infamous, "How was school today?" And they can sometimes get lost during the nightly homework and bath-time routine. I realize that the idea of spending even more time with your child as he gets older is not very practical—his schedule gets more hectic, and life just seems to get busier and busier—yet it is important to keep as a goal. We tend to think that when our children get older they need us less, yet in reality they need us even more to serve as a guide they can refer to while navigating a complicated and complex world. During this stage being a good listener is the best gift we can give our growing children.

Another characteristic of children in Stage III of their social and emotional development is an acute awareness of all things fair and unfair. This is particularly valuable for parents to know because any discrepancies between your expectations for your child and your own behavior will *not* go unnoticed. One example of how this manifested itself in our home was when my oldest daughter was going through a phase of being particularly critical of herself. We spoke about how it is just as harmful to give yourself put-downs as it is to give other people put-downs. She immediately reminded me of a time when we were looking at family photographs and I made a comment about how I did not like the way I looked in the picture. Although I cringed inside, I realized that she was right. I often give myself put-downs in front of her—modeling the exact behavior that I wanted my daughter to avoid. I acknowledged that she was right, and we both made a pact to not be so critical of ourselves.

Developing good social skills and healthy ways of managing emotions can be challenging for children and adults alike. As parents, there is a lot we can do to help our children navigate their way, and we can often learn a thing or two about ourselves as well.

PUT-UPS AND PUT-DOWNS

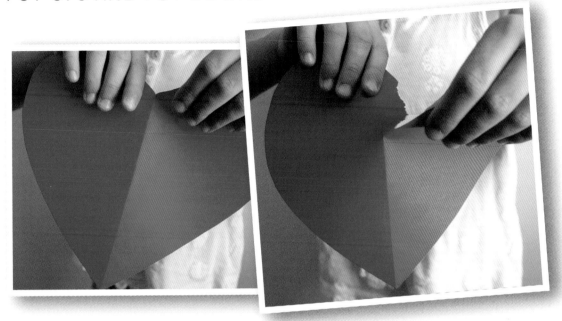

If I could choose two phrases to be introduced into every household and school across the land, they would be "put-ups" and "put-downs." Simply stated, put-downs are words or actions that make people feel bad, and put-ups are words or actions that make people feel good.[3] They are simple concepts to teach, and the impact can be profound; in fact, these are two of the most powerful concepts I have ever taught in the classroom or to my own children. Equipping your child with a deep understanding of these terms gives him the ability to communicate feelings, which may have seemed almost intangible before. The language of put-ups and put-downs provides your child with the skills needed to speak up for himself as well as to stand up for others.

This lesson has been adapted from *Connected and Respected K–2* by Ken Breeding and Jane Harrison.

> **Materials**
>
> Two large hearts cut out of colored paper
>
> Susie's Day printable (see page 244)

ONE STEP AHEAD

For this activity to have the greatest impact, your child needs to be able relate to the occurrences that take place in Susie's Day. Before you share this experience with your child, read the story provided and make changes as needed so it will be relevant to your child's life. An example may be that your child has lockers instead of cubbies, or you may change the main character to a boy. Feel free to add events that you know your child has dealt with in the past.

THE PROCESS

Start out by asking your child if he can tell you what a "put-down" is. Although many children have never heard the phrase before, they usually can grasp the meaning quickly. Ask him to give you examples of put-downs he has heard. Next ask him if he can tell you what "put-up" means. When he comprehends the meaning, ask him to give you some examples.

Show your child one of the large paper hearts you cut out, and tell him that it belongs to a girl named Susie. Explain that you are going to read him a story about Susie's day, and he should watch the heart to see how put-ups or put-downs makes a person feel.

As you read the story, stop to rip off a piece of the paper heart after each put-down (put-downs are in italics). By the end of the story, you should have one small piece of Susie's heart left in your hand. This really hits home with children, so be sure to tell your child that he will have a chance to mend Susie's heart. (See the Susie's Day printable.)

After reading the story, invite your child to change the put-downs into put-ups. Ask him if he can think of different actions or behaviors that would change the way Susie felt. For example, Michael could nicely say, "Excuse me, I need to get to my cubby, Susie." Encourage your child to think of alternatives for each put-down in the story, and then reread it incorporating his ideas.

When you are finished reading the revised story, take out the second heart and congratulate your child on making Susie's heart feel happy again. Point out how powerful words and actions can be, and suggest that your child pay attention to whether he is giving put-ups or put-downs through his words and actions.

> **Books to Inspire**
>
> *Chrysanthemum* by Kevin Henkes
>
> *The Hundred Dresses* by Eleanor Estes
>
> *The Quarreling Book* by Charlotte Zolotow
>
> *Snail Started It!* by Katja Reider and Angela von Roehl

I would like to end with a word of caution. Be prepared to be told occasionally by your child, "What you just said feels like a put-down." He has learned his lesson, and this is where your learning comes in. When this happens in our home, I simply take a deep breath and do what I ask of my children, which is to rethink what I want to say and rephrase it without the tone or the subtle dig. It can be humbling at times, but the result is a powerful foundation of respect within the family.

MORE TO EXPLORE

Begin to include the terms "put-ups" and "put-downs" in your daily conversations. Point out to your child when you hear someone in your family giving a put-down, and together brainstorm ways of saying the same thing differently so that it does not feel so negative. On the same note, point out the put-ups that you hear your child giving or receiving. You will be amazed at how quickly children begin to integrate this concept into their hearts and minds.

You can also make a difference by volunteering to do this activity in your child's class in place of reading a story. The children really love the experience, and it is one of the best gifts you can give to your child and his teacher.

WHAT IS A MISUNDERSTANDING?

It helps children to place a label on a misunderstanding when it occurs. A misunderstanding can be one of the most frustrating situations for

Materials

Misunderstandings print-
able (see page 245)

young children, and they often are not able to see beyond
the angry feelings that arise. If a grown-up can help her
identify and label a situation, your child can start the communication process that is necessary for deciphering where
and how the misunderstanding occurred.

ONE STEP AHEAD

To prepare, have a few examples in mind of misunderstandings you have
had in the past to share with your child during this experience.

THE PROCESS

Start by reading *Nobody Likes Me!* by Raoul Krischanitz or any other book
that incorporates a misunderstanding into the story line. When you are
finished reading the story, talk with your child about how the dog mis-
understands all of the other animals' responses to him. Explore how the
misunderstandings affected the dog.

After some discussion ask your child if she has ever had a misunderstanding with someone. You can explain that a misunderstanding is
when you think someone did, said, or thought something, but they really
did, said, or thought something else. Be sure to contribute your own
experiences with misunderstandings to the conversation.

Ask your child to choose one misunderstanding to draw and write
about, and provide her with the Misunderstandings printable. You can

select a misunderstanding to record as well. Spending time drawing and writing together provides a great opportunity to continue the conversation in a fun and lighthearted context.

MORE TO EXPLORE

Now that you have begun to explore the concept of misunderstandings with your child, it helps to identify them when they happen. Explicitly naming misunderstandings as they occur will help your child begin to correctly label them as they pop up in her own life.

FAMILY PUPPET THEATER: ADVENTURES IN ROLE-PLAYING

Role-playing is a very effective tool that can help children work through some of the difficult situations they encounter in their social lives. Acting out a variety of scenarios in a safe environment allows your child to gain a fresh perspective on challenging moments and teaches her strategies for

Materials

Large wooden Popsicle sticks

Photos of family and friends

Puppet-making materials: glue, fabric, and embellishments

A place for role-playing (puppet theater, edge of a bed, behind a couch)

Role-Playing Scenarios printable (see page 246)

handling similar situations in the future. These exercises will also encourage your child to consider multiple perspectives, an essential skill for effective conflict resolution.

ONE STEP AHEAD

Write down examples ahead of time of social situations that your child has experienced at school or at home and incorporate them into the role-playing scenarios. The more relevant the role-plays are to your child, the more meaningful this experience will be.

To prepare for this activity, copy and cut out the Role-Playing Scenarios printable. It adds a mysterious element if you fold the scenarios and put them in a basket so your child can select them one at a time without knowing what comes next.

THE PROCESS

Start out by making puppets together of your family members. You can use any puppets for role-playing activities, although it adds a unique dimension when the puppets are friends and loved ones. For example, my girls used puppets of my sister and me to role-play situations in which two siblings have a disagreement. We made our puppets by cutting out pictures of loved ones and gluing them onto large Popsicle sticks. The girls then used fabric scraps to make clothes for each person.

Explain that you are going to play a game where you and your child will act out different situations. Let your child know that some of the stories may present problems, and it would be great if she could come up with some ideas on how to solve them.

Invite your child to pick a scenario out of the basket and then read the situation to her. Next decide who will play which part. If just you and your child are participating, you can each take a role; if you have more than one child, encourage them all to join in.

After the situation has been acted out, ask some guiding questions (see the bottom of the Role-Playing Scenarios printable). Discuss different possibilities for more positive outcomes, and ask your child to act it out again incorporating her ideas.

Leave the family puppets out for your child to use any time she likes. It is remarkable to see how often she will play with them. If you quietly listen in on her imaginary play, you can gain insight into some of the questions and issues your child may be dealing with. This is a wonderful way for your child to independently make sense of and work through a variety of circumstances she may face.

FEELING PEACEFUL

For your child to aspire toward living a peaceful life, he needs to be able to identify when he is and is not experiencing peace. This activity helps your child define for himself the true meaning of peace. It also sets the stage for "A Place for Peace," a project that comes later in this chapter.

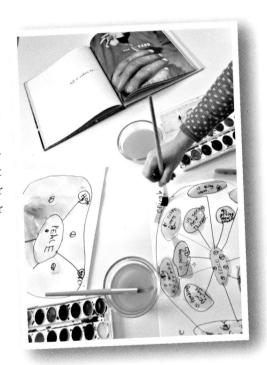

Materials

A variety of musical instruments or any noise-making objects (pots, pans, and wooden spoons work well)

Drawing paper

A permanent fine-point black marker

Watercolor paints

ONE STEP AHEAD

Think of some examples of when you feel peaceful to share with our child as you embark on this experience together.

THE PROCESS

To make the feeling of peace tangible to your child, gather a bunch of musical instruments or other noisemakers. Explain that you are going to explore what it means to feel peaceful. Encourage your whole family to participate, and make sure that each person has at least one instrument. Next ask everyone to play their instrument as loud as they can.

When you are finished, ask your family to describe the experience. Some questions you can ask are:

- What are some words that describe that experience?
- What are some of the feelings you experienced?
- Did we work together to make our sounds?
- How would our noises be different if we worked together?

Repeat the same activity, but this time have family members try to complement the sounds others are making. Compare and contrast both experiences. Point out that when people work together, it makes for a more peaceful environment.

Next ask your child to come up with other times in his life when he has felt peaceful. We read *A Little Peace* by Barbara Kerley for an added dose of inspiration.

> **Books to Inspire**
>
> *Can You Say Peace?* by Karen Katz
>
> *A Little Peace* by Barbara Kerley
>
> *The Peace Book* by Todd Parr
>
> *What Does Peace Feel Like?* by Vladimir Radunsky and children from all over the world

You may want to introduce the concept of brainstorming, which is coming up with many ideas or thoughts about a topic. Show your child that he can put the main idea, which is "peace," in the center of his paper with a circle around it, and then connect any thoughts about peace he may have to it. Younger children can dictate their words to you or draw pictures. Your child can use any art materials he likes for this project; for example, using a permanent black marker for writing and drawing and then using watercolor paints over the top always turns out lovely.

MORE TO EXPLORE

Save your child's peace painting to hang in the place for peace you build together. (We'll build it later in this chapter in "A Place for Peace.") Your conversations with your child about what it means to feel peaceful will help you define your special place.

ABCs OF CONFLICT RESOLUTION

The benefit of learning how to effectively resolve conflicts will last a lifetime. Children are often told to resolve conflicts on their own, but are not explicitly taught the proper skills to do so successfully. This experience, which comes from *Connected and Respected* by Ken Breeding and Jane Harrison, outlines simple steps children can take to work through conflicts on their own.

Materials

A picture book that contains a conflict between two characters (see a list of recommendations in "Books to Inspire")

ABCs of Resolving Conflicts printable (see page 247)

ONE STEP AHEAD

Plan ahead by thinking about some meaningful objects you might include in your family's peaceful space that represent positive feelings for your child. Some examples are family photos, stuffed animals, or beloved rocks and shells.

THE PROCESS

Introduce your child to the idea of creating a special place where everyone in the family can go to feel peaceful. Ask her if she would like to choose and build a place for peace in your home. Involve your child in the whole process of selecting a space and decorations for the peace place.

You can build on the momentum by suggesting that your child make a sign that lists the things she would like to do in the space (see the Our Peace Place printable). This is an important step; your family's place for peace needs to be a space where your child wants to go for a variety of reasons, such as relaxing, reading, talking, playing, *and* resolving conflicts. If it is solely used for resolving conflicts, it will begin to feel like a consequence or time-out place, which defeats the purpose.

Spend time together creating your special new place. Invite your child to add items that will make it feel cozy and that have sentimental value. Hang your child's sign, her ABCs of conflict resolution, and her peaceful paintings nearby so she can refer to them as needed.

> **Books to Inspire**
>
> *Peaceful Piggy Meditation* by Kerry Lee MacLean
>
> *A Quiet Place* by Douglas Wood

MORE TO EXPLORE

Openness on your part to participate in the peace place will go a long way with your child. Remember to use the space for a variety of special moments; for example, it is a great place to share some precious one-on-one time.

When your child faces conflicts outside the home, remind her of the skills she uses in your family's peaceful place. She will eventually learn to apply the same techniques for conflict resolution to situations she encounters in her everyday life.

PREDICTING THE FUTURE: EXPLORING CAUSE AND EFFECT

Predicting the future is a wonderful activity to share as a family. Everyone brings his or her own perspectives and personal experiences, which makes for great discussions and enriches the overall experience. This learning event is a fun way to encourage your child to think about the effects of his own behavior as well as the behavior of others.

> *Materials*
>
> Any props that can playfully be used to "tell the future," such as rocks, crystals, balls, or tea leaves
>
> Dress-up items that a fortune-teller might wear (scarves, hats, and so on)
>
> Predicting the Future printable (see page 249)

ONE STEP AHEAD

This activity is most valuable if it includes situations that are personally relevant to your child. Look over the scenarios included in the Predicting the Future printable. Print and cut out the scenarios you'd like to use. It adds a bit more drama if you fold up the scenarios and place them in a basket or a bag. Add any situations that relate specifically to issues your child may be currently struggling with.

THE PROCESS

> **Books to Inspire**
>
> *The Fortune-Tellers* by Lloyd Alexander
>
> *Forty Fortunes: A Tale of Iran* by Aaron Shepard

If your child does not know what a fortune-teller is, offer him a simple explanation. It's fun to read one of the books listed to the left to set the stage and get him excited about this activity.

Suggest that your child assume the role of a fortune-teller and try to predict the future. Generate some ideas of props he could use to become a fortune-teller. Once he is appropriately attired, ask him to pick a scenario from the basket and make a prediction (answer the question).[4]

Take turns and encourage every member of the family to participate in foreseeing the future.

MORE TO EXPLORE

You can incorporate the concepts behind this activity into your child's daily life. Keep out one of the props you used, and suggest that your child "look into the crystal" or "put on his fortune-telling hat" when he needs to view a certain action or situation from a new perspective.

DO YOU NEED IT OR DO YOU WANT IT?

Children need to maintain a healthy perspective about material objects. When I introduced my daughters to books that depicted children around the world (see "Building a Multicultural Library"), I noticed that they made comments about what a certain child had or did not have. Along with exposing the girls to cultures all over the world, I realized that I needed to broaden their definition of what a *want* is versus a *need*. After engag-

ing in this learning experience together, it completely changed our discussions about children
across the globe. Rather than looking at what
a child did or did not have, they noticed what
was unique about the child's everyday experiences. Incorporating the language of wants versus needs into her conversations will also help
to keep your child in check when it comes to her
desires for personal possessions.

> **Materials**
>
> Blank index cards
>
> A variety of children's
>   magazines and
>   catalogues
>
> Wants and Needs
>   printable (see
>   page 250)

ONE STEP AHEAD

When preparing for this activity, consider some
of your child's most recent "wantings." With that in mind look through
magazines and catalogues and cut out pictures of things that you know
your child wants and things she needs. Some examples of wants might
be toys, "cool" clothes, jewelry, music, and games. Some needs might be
food, basic clothing, and shelter. Glue each picture onto a blank index
card and have them ready.

Be prepared for your own internal struggles during this activity. Yes,
shelter is a necessity, but at what point does it become a luxury? The
same question goes for food, clothes, and so on and so forth. Are music,
books, art, and family outings wants or needs? These are all questions
that came up for us as a family. Although they are not easy to answer, the
conversation is well worth having together.

THE PROCESS

It helps to introduce this experience with a relevant story or book. We used
Fly Away Home by Eve Bunting, which is a about a boy who lives in an air-
port with his father. If you feel that your child is too young or not ready
to handle the topic of homelessness, flipping through *Material World: A
Global Family Portrait* by Peter Menzel will inspire a great discussion.

When you feel the time is right, ask your child what items she thinks
are things she needs (things that she needs to survive) versus what things
she thinks she wants (things that would be nice, but that she could do
without).

Next, share the index cards that you prepared along with the Wants
and Needs printable. Ask your child to place each index card you give her

in either the wants or the needs column. Discuss the reasons behind each choice she makes.

When you have finished exploring all the cards, invite your child to find her own examples of wants and needs by selecting and cutting out pictures from magazines. Then she can glue them in the appropriate column of the printable.

MORE TO EXPLORE

There are many wonderful books that offer children glimpses into the lives of children all over the world. I provide a list of our family favorites under "Growing Globally" in the resource section. By reading books together that present multicultural perspectives, you can keep the conversation going and continue to positively expand your child's view of the world.

MAKING A DIFFERENCE: OPPORTUNITIES FOR COMMUNITY SERVICE

Children are natural advocates and love making a positive impact on the world around them. You can channel this enthusiasm by providing outlets for your child to express his views and work toward positive change. Rather than feeling overwhelmed, scared, or helpless when confronted by life's injustices, your child will come away empowered and confident in his ability to do good and create change.

ONE STEP AHEAD

Listen to your child to pick up on the things that really matter to him. If he notices a lot of trash on his favorite beach, suggest that he plan a beach cleanup. If he loves bird-watching, encourage him to check out the Audubon Society Web site for ways to protect migrating birds. If he overhears some distressing news that upsets him, try to find a way for him to help the situation, such as donating items to victims of an earthquake. Although these gestures may seem small, they teach your child that he can make a difference in the areas that matter most to him.

THE PROCESS

When your child contributes to his community and the world, he learns that small acts can have a big impact and that by giving he can become a part of something larger than himself. Once he feels it—truly internalizes the feeling of making a difference—he will begin to seek it out on his own and expect nothing less from himself and others.

Below is a list of some avenues for your child to explore, to express his views and make a positive difference in the world.

TAKE ACTION

There are a number of simple and tangible actions that your child can take to make a difference on a local level for his community. Here are a few of our favorites.

- Collect food and deliver it to a local food pantry
- Plant a tree in your state
- Plan a local beach or park cleanup or volunteer through the National Park Service
- Brighten someone's day by making cards or pictures that can be delivered by your local Meals on Wheels
- Donate gently used toys; involve your children in the selection process and go together to deliver them to Goodwill

WRITE LETTERS

A wonderful way for your child to feel that she has a voice is to write letters to the president and members of other branches of government about the issues that she cares about most. Your child is likely to receive a response, which adds a satisfying dimension to the experience.

- Contact the White House
- Write your senator
- Write your representative

RAISE MONEY

Children are entrepreneurs at heart. There are many ways for children to raise money, ranging from selling lemonade to doing chores around

. . . .
List Paper

Date

Date

Date

NURTURING YOUNG AUTHORS

Alphabet Chart

Aa Bb Cc Dd Ee Ff Gg Hh Ii Jj Kk Ll Mm
Nn Oo Pp Qq Rr Ss Tt Uu Vv Ww Xx Yy Zz

1 2 3 4 5 6 7 8 9 10

Aa Bb Cc Dd Ee Ff Gg Hh Ii Jj Kk Ll Mm
Nn Oo Pp Qq Rr Ss Tt Uu Vv Ww Xx Yy Zz

1 2 3 4 5 6 7 8 9 10

PRINTABLES

IN THE FOLLOWING SECTION I have provided resources that will help make the learning experiences in this book simple, successful, and meaningful. You can use the following printables as is or adapt them to meet the specific needs of your family. You are free to photocopy the printables from this book for your own personal use. PDFs of these worksheets are also available to download at www.playfullearning.net and at www.shambhala.com/playfullearning.

....
Story Paper 1

Date _____

Story Paper 2

Date _____

Story Paper 3

Date _____

Story Paper 4

Story Paper 5

Letter Paper 1

Dear _____ ,

Love,

_____

Letter Paper 2

_____

Dear _____ ,

_____

_____

Love,

_____

....

Letter Paper 3

_____

Dear _____ ,

_____

_____

_____

_____

_____

Love,

_____

THE JOY OF READING

....

Alphabet Cards

Ff	Ll	Rr	Xx	
Ee	Kk	Qq	Ww	
Dd	Jj	Pp	Vv	
Cc	Ii	Oo	Uu	
Bb	Hh	Nn	Tt	Zz
Aa	Gg	Mm	Ss	Yy

Build-a-Word Set 1

a   t   p   c

b   g   m   s

cat   bag   mat

sat   cap   map

Build-a-Word Set 2

b   u   r   g   h

j   t   d   n

bug   bud   rug

jug   hug   nut

Build-a-Word Set 3

ll   e   n   t

g   w   b   m

bell   wet   net

web   gem

Build-a-Word Set 4

g   t   m   p

o   d   p

dog   pot   pop

top   mop

Build-a-Word Set 5

x   p   s   g

l   z   i   d

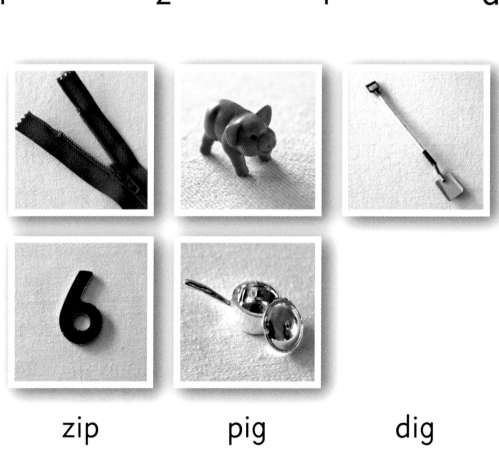

zip   pig   dig

six   lid

MATHEMATICIANS AT WORK

Clip Math

1 ●	2 ●●
3 ●●●	4 ●●●●

5

● ● ● ● ●

6

● ● ● ● ● ●

7

● ● ● ● ● ● ●

8

● ● ● ● ● ● ● ●

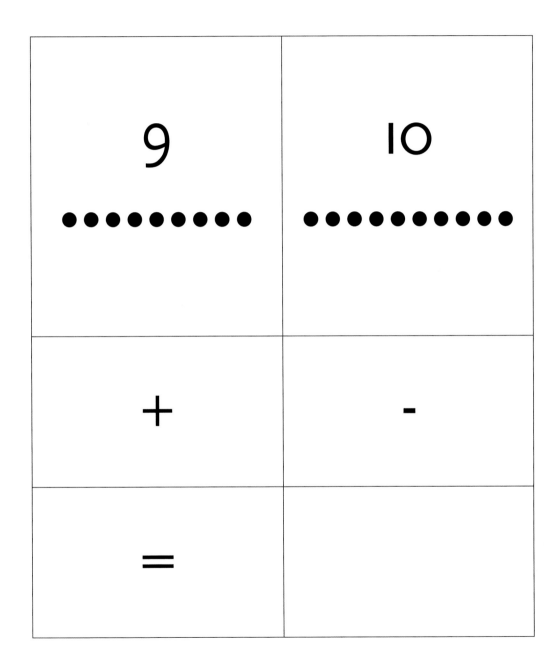

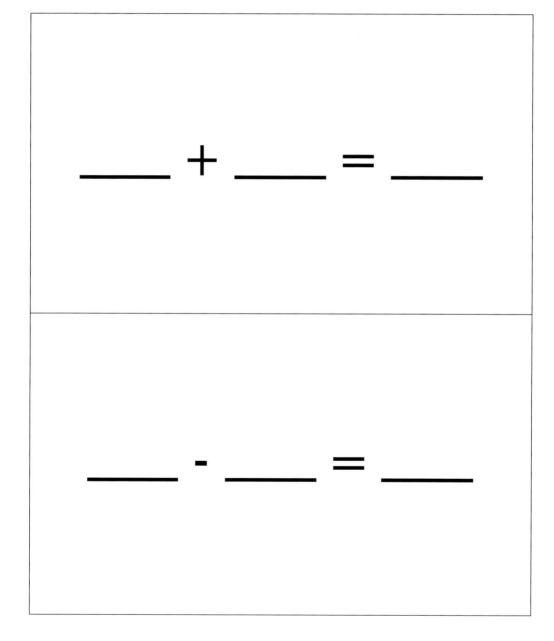

Number Line

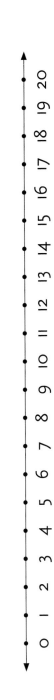

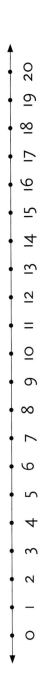

Number Cards

5	10
4	9
3	8
2	7
1	6

Seashore Story Problems

You have found 3 shells on your walk. Then you found 2 more. How many shells do you have altogether?

After finding 4 shells you discover 3 more near the water. How many shells do you have altogether?

As you were walking along the shore, you discovered a group of 5 shells and then you uncovered 2 more. How many shells do you have in total?

You found 6 shells and your sister found 4. How many do you have altogether?

On your walk you collected 8 shells. Then you accidently dropped 2. How many do you have left?

At the beach you collected 10 shells. You give your grandma 5 of your favorites. How many shells are left in your collection?

Math Equations

5 + 5 =	4 + 3 =
1 + 2 =	5 + 3 =
1 + 3 =	4 + 6 =
2 + 2 =	3 + 3 =
2 + 3 =	4 + 4 =
4 + 2 =	7 + 2 =

Blank Math Equations

___ + ___ = ___	___ + ___ = ___
___ + ___ = ___	___ + ___ = ___
___ + ___ = ___	___ - ___ = ___
___ - ___ = ___	___ - ___ = ___
___ - ___ = ___	___ - ___ = ___

My Pebble Graph

10					
9					
8					
7					
6					
5					
4					
3					
2					
1					
	Orange	Gray	White	Brown	Many

My Candy Graph

10					
9					
8					
7					
6					
5					
4					
3					
2					
1					
	Orange	Yellow	Brown	Red	Other

Sorting and Classifying 1

Sorting and Classifying 2

Sorting and Classifying 3

Types of Patterns

Types of Patterns	Linear (Repeating)	Symmetry
Branching	Spirals	Tessellations

Linear	Linear	Linear
Symmetry	Symmetry	Symmetry
Branching	Branching	Branching
Spirals	Spirals	Spirals
Tessellations	Tessellations	Tessellations

LEGO Measurements

Things that are approximately the same length as

1. _____

2. _____

3. _____

4. _____

Things that are approximately the same length as

1. _____

2. _____

3. _____

4. _____

Body Measurements

	Estimate	Length	Difference

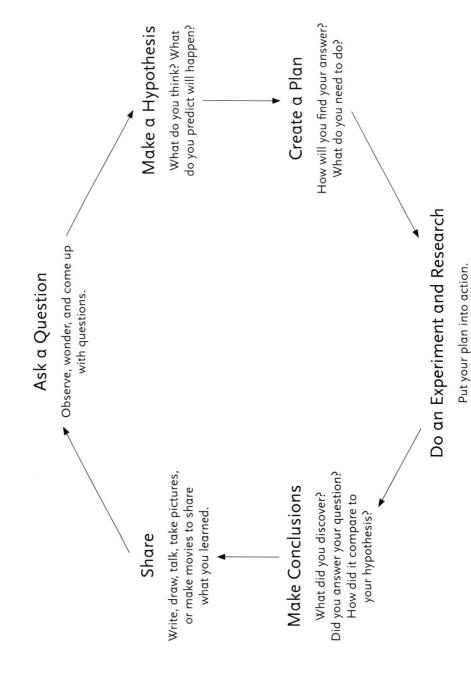

The Scientific Process

Ask a Question
Observe, wonder, and come up with questions.

Make a Hypothesis
What do you think? What do you predict will happen?

Create a Plan
How will you find your answer? What do you need to do?

Do an Experiment and Research
Put your plan into action. Explain what you did and how you did it.

Make Conclusions
What did you discover? Did you answer your question? How did it compare to your hypothesis?

Share
Write, draw, talk, take pictures, or make movies to share what you learned.

....

Science Journal 1

Hypothesis	Conclusion

Hypothesis	Conclusion

Science Journal 2

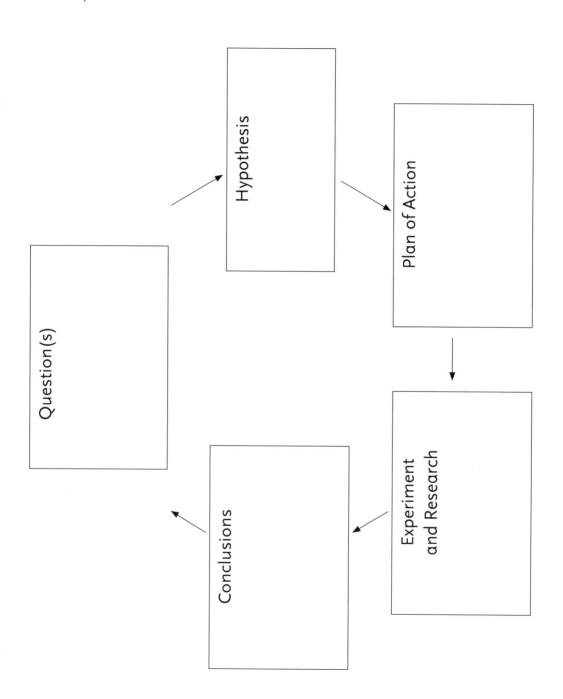

Question(s)

Hypothesis

Plan of Action

Experiment and Research

Conclusions

The Water Cycle

Phases of the Moon

Phases of the Moon

Waxing
Crescent

New Moon

Waning
Crescent

First
Quarter

Third Quarter

Waxing
Gibbous

Full Moon

Waning
Gibbous

Cloud Formations

Cumulus

Cirrus

Stratus

Parts of a Bean Seed

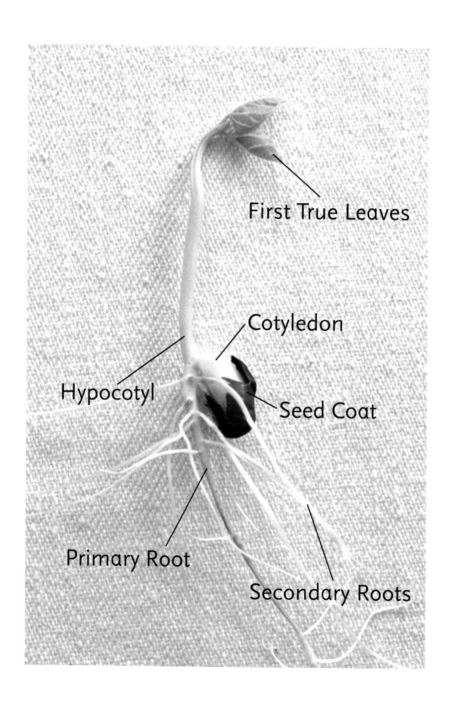

Parts of a Flower 1

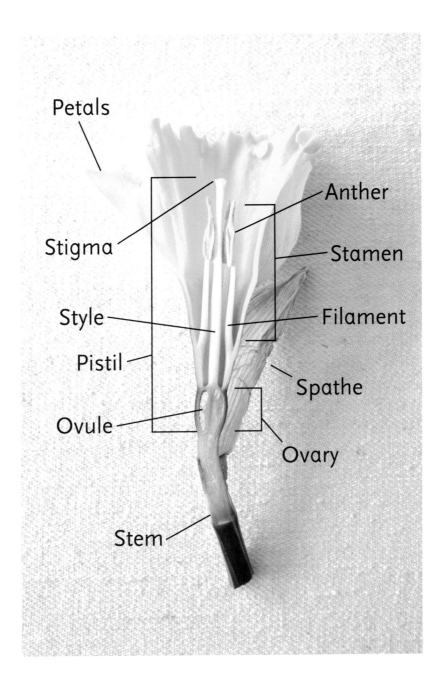

Petals

Anther

Stigma

Stamen

Style

Filament

Pistil

Spathe

Ovule

Ovary

Stem

Parts of a Flower 2

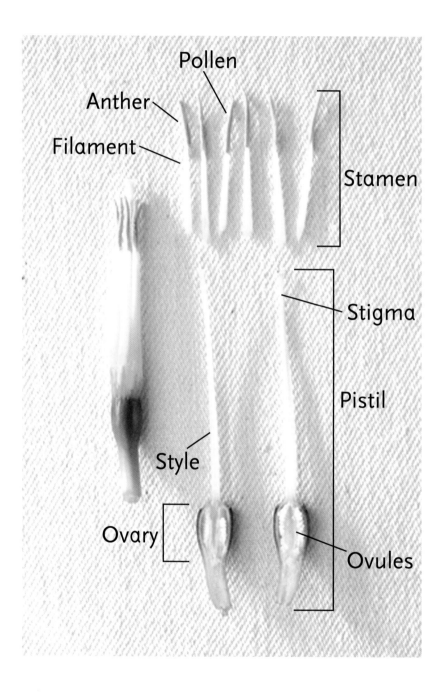

Looking Closely at Bark

List four words that describe your bark.

_____   _____

_____   _____

Leaf Veins

Pinnate

Parallel

Palmate

GROWING GLOBALLY

Can You Find It?

Item	Location	✓

Who Lives Here?

Coordinates	Name(s)

Map Key

Key

RAISING THE CITIZENS OF TOMORROW
....
Susie's Day

Susie comes into her classroom in the morning excited about the day. When she goes to put her lunch in her cubby, she kneels in front of Mike's cubby. Mike comes by and pushes her to the side and yells, *"Hey, get out of my way. I can't get to my cubby!"*

As the children begin to sit on the rug for morning meeting, Susie starts to sit down next to another girl in her class named Melissa. *Melissa makes a face and says, "I'm saving this place for my friend."*

At lunchtime Susie goes to sit at a table with some of the girls in her class. *When she sits down, they all turn their backs toward her and start talking quietly to each other.*

During recess Susie can't find anything to do and sits back to watch the other children playing. When she finally works up enough courage to ask a group if she can play with them they say, *"This is a game for only three people."*

At the end of the day when Susie's mom picks her up from school she asks, "So how was your day Susie?"

What do you think she said?

Misunderstandings

Draw a picture of a time that you experienced a misunderstanding.

Describe the misunderstanding.

_____

_____

_____

_____

Role-Playing Scenarios

Sarah and Tiffany love to play together. One day Sarah wanted to play checkers and Tiffany wanted to play a card game. They started to yell at each other, and then they both started crying and ran into different rooms.	Emma and Michael were working on drawings for their books that they wrote. Emma was using the green pencil. Michael told Emma that he needed it, and she said, "No." Michael grabbed the pencil out of Emma's hand and they started arguing.
John had been building a big castle with blocks. Heather was playing with her jump rope and accidently knocked over a few blocks. Heather did not say anything and kept jumping rope. John got upset and started yelling at her. Heather yelled back at John.	Billy and Ann have been friends since kindergarten. One day when they were on the playground, Billy wanted to play with some new friends. Ann told Billy that if he played with other people it meant that he was not her friend.
Ashley and Ryan had been working hard on their paintings. When Ashley got up to get a snack, Ryan accidently spilled juice on Ashley's work. When Ashley came back she saw that her painting had been ruined. She asked Ryan, "What happened?" and he said, "I don't know."	Susan was at the park with her mom. As she was playing on the swings, a girl came up to her and asked if she wanted to play on the monkey bars. Susan felt shy and said, "No." The girl walked away feeling sad.

Guiding Questions
- What happened in this situation?
- What is the conflict?
- How does _____ feel? How does _____ feel?
- How could they have prevented this conflict from happening?
- How can they resolve this conflict?
- Can you role-play this situation again and either prevent or resolve the conflict?

ABCs of Resolving Conflicts

A _____

B _____

C _____

D _____

A Ask, "What is the problem?"
B Brainstorm some ideas for solving the problem.
C Choose the best idea.
D Do it.

Adapted from Breeding, Ken and Harrison, Jane. *Connected and Respected Grades K–2.*

Our Peace Place
is for...

_____

_____

_____

_____

Predicting the Future

What will happen if you do not say "hello" back to a person who says it to you?	What will happen if you do not say "please" and "thank you" to people?
What will happen if you share with your friends?	What will happen if you put people down?
Bobby and Adam are playing with their race cars. By accident Bobby breaks the tire off of Adam's car when he is not looking. When Adam discovers that his car is broken, he asks Bobby, "What happened?" Bobby says, "I don't know." What will happen the next time they play together?	Joe loves to play soccer. During recess he watches the other children play, but he does not participate because he is afraid the other kids will laugh at him. What will happen if he does the same thing everyday?
Emma's kindergarten class always has to clean up their room before they can go outside for recess. Emma decides that she doesn't want to help so she asks if she can go to the bathroom every day during cleanup. How will Emma's teacher and friends feel?	Sarah and Lily are drawing pictures together. Sarah asks Lily if she can use her coloring book. Lily says, "Yes," and lets Sarah pick out the picture she would like to color. What will happen the next time they play together?

Wants and Needs

Needs	
Wants	

Notes

Introduction

1. Kathy Hirsh-Pasek, Roberta Michnick Golinkoff, Laura E. Berk, and Dorothy G. Singer, *A Mandate for Playful Learning in Preschool: Presenting the Evidence* (New York: Oxford University Press, 2009), 29.
2. Tina Blythe and Associates, *The Teaching for Understanding Guide* (San Francisco: Jossey-Bass Publishers, 1998), 12.

Chapter 1. Nurturing Young Authors

1. Lucy McCormick Calkins, *The Art of Teaching Writing* (Portsmouth, New Hampshire: Heinemann, 1994), 21.

Chapter 2. The Joy of Reading

1. Emma Walton Hamilton, *Raising Bookworms: Getting Kids Reading for Pleasure and Empowerment* (Sag Harbor, N.Y.: Beach Tree Books, 2009), 16.
2. Stephanie Harvey and Anne Goudvis, *Strategies That Work* (New York: Stenhouse Publishers, 2000), 70.
3. Donald R. Bear, Marcia Invernizzi, Shane Templeton, and Francine Johnston, *Words Their Way: Word Study for Phonics, Vocabulary, and Spelling Instruction* (Upper Saddle River, N.J.: Merrill, 2000), 121.

Chapter 3. Mathematicians at Work

1. The National Association for the Education of Young Children, "Early Childhood Mathematics: Promoting Good Beginnings" (2002), 3.
2. Mary Baratta-Lorton, *Workjobs II* (Parsippany, New Jersey: Dale Seymour Publications, 1979), 6.
3. Ibid., 6.
4. Marilyn Burns, *About Teaching Mathematics: A K–8 Resource* (Sausalito, Calif.: Math Solutions Publications, 2000), 25.
5. Mary Baratta-Lorton, *Workjobs II* (Parsippany, New Jersey: Dale Seymour Publications, 1979), 6.
6. Mary Baratta-Lorton, *Workjobs* (Parsippany, New Jersey: Dale Seymour Publications, 1972), 167.
7. Marilyn Burns, *Math and Literature (K–3) Book One* (Sausalito, Calif.: Math Solutions Publications, 1992), 19.
8. Mary Baratta-Lorton, *Workjobs II* (Parsippany, New Jersey: Dale Seymour Publications, 1979), 90.
9. Mary Baratta-Lorton, *Workjobs* (Parsippany, New Jersey: Dale Seymour Publications, 1972), 203.
10. Ibid., 169.
11. Marilyn Burns, *Math and Literature (K–3) Book One* (Sausalito, Calif.: Math Solutions Publications, 1992), 47.

Chapter 4. Scientific Investigations

1. Stephane Bearce, *A Kid's Guide to Making a Terrarium* (Hockessin, Delaware: Mitchell Lane Publishers, 2010), 16.
2. Joseph Cornell, *Sharing Nature with Children* (Nevada City, N.J.: Dawn Publications, 1979), 27.

Chapter 5. Exploration of Art and Artists

1. Howard Gardner, *Art Education and Human Development* (Los Angeles: The J. Paul Getty Museum, 1990), 16.
2. Ibid., 16.
3. Nancy R. Smith, *Experience and Art* (New York: Teachers College Press, 1993), 18.
4. Ibid., 28.
5. Ibid., 36.
6. Ibid., 72.
7. Sabbath, Carol. *Monet and the Impressionists for Kids* (Chicago: Chicago Review Press, 2002), 21.

Chapter 6. Growing Globally

1. Marcelo M. Suárez-Orozco and Desirée Baolian Qin-Hilliard, eds., *Globalization: Culture and Education in the New Millennium* (Berkeley: University of California Press and Ross Institute, 2004), 4.
2. David Sobel, *Mapmaking with Children* (Portsmouth, New Hampshire: Heinemann, 1949), 22.
3. Ibid., 17.

Chapter 7. Raising the Citizens of Tomorrow

1. Linda Lantiera, introduction by Daniel Goleman, *Techniques to Cultivate Inner Strength in Children: Building Emotional Intelligence* (Boulder: Sounds True, 2008), 2.
2. Ken Breeding and Jane Harrison, *Connected and Respected* (Cambridge, Mass.: Educators for Social Responsibility, 2007), 11.
3. Ibid., 99.
4. Judith Anne Rice, *The Kindness Curriculum: Introducing Young Children to Loving Values* (St. Paul, Minn.: Readleaf Press, 1995), 57.

Resource Guide

THIS SECTION LISTS books, Web sites, and other resources that will enhance your family's experience with the activities in this book. My daughters and I found many of the titles mentioned here at our local library. I can't emphasize enough what a wonderful tool children's books have been in introducing my girls to meaningful learning opportunities. Books can capture a child's attention and pique her interest in a topic when prompting from a grown-up fails. I have also included the curriculum and theory books that inspired many of the Playful Learning experiences in this book. I highly recommend them to anyone who would like to delve deeper into a particular topic.

How to Use Playful Learning

Blythe, Tina, and Associates. *The Teaching for Understanding Guide*. San Francisco: Jossey-Bass Publishers, 1998.

Playful Learning Spaces

Casely, Judith. *Dear Annie*. New York: Greenwillow Books, 1991.
Keats, Jack Ezra. *A Letter to Amy*. New York: Viking, 1968.

Owen, Ann. *Delivering Your Mail: A Book about Mail Carriers*. Minneapolis: Picture Window Books, 2004.

MATERIALS

Large archival storage boxes, Gaylord (www.gaylord.com),
Portfolios for student work, Dick Blick Art Materials (www.dickblick.com),

Nurturing Young Authors

Ahlberg, Janet, and Allen Ahlberg. *The Jolly Postman or Other People's Letters*. New York: Little, Brown and Company, 1986.
Bottner, Barbara, and Gerald Kruglik. *Wallace's Lists*. New York: Katherine Tegen Books, 2004.
Boynton, Sandra. *If at First…* Boston: Little, Brown and Company, 1980.
Brown, Susan Taylor. *Oliver's Must-Do List*. Honesdale: Boyd Mills Press, Inc., 2005.
Calkins, Lucy McCormick. *The Art of Teaching Writing*. Portsmouth, New Hampshire: Heinemann, 1994.
Carle, Eric. *Have You Seen My Cat?* New York: Little Simon, 1987.
Cowley, Joy. *Mrs. Wishy-Washy Makes a Splash!* New York: Philomel Books, 1993.
Durant, Alan. *Dear Tooth Fairy*. Cambridge, Mass.: Candlewick Press, 2003.
Ewald, Wendy. *Secret Games: Collaborative Works with Children 1969–1999*. Berlin: Scalo Zurich, 2000.
———. *The Best Part of Me: Children Talk about Their Bodies in Pictures and Words*. Boston: Little, Brown and Company, 2002.
Fanelli, Sara. *My Map Book*. New York: HarperCollins Publishers, 1995.
Fox, Mem. *Wilfrid Gordon McDonald Partridge*. Brooklyn: Kane/Miller Book Publishers, 1985.
Gertsein, Mordicai. *A Book*. New York: Henry Holt and Company, 2009.
Ginsberg, Mirra. *The Chick and the Duckling*. New York: Aladdin Books, 1986.
Heard, Georgia. *Awakening the Heart: Exploring Poetry in Elementary and Middle School*. Portsmouth, New Hampshire: Heinemann, 1998.
Hobbie, Holly. *Toot and Puddle*. Boston, Mass.: Little, Brown and Company, 1997.
James, Simon. *Dear Mr. Blueberry*. New York: Margaret K. McElderry Books, 1991.
Lionni, Leo. *Let's Play*. New York: Alfred A. Knopf, 2003.
Martin Jr., Bill. *Brown Bear, Brown Bear, What Do You See?* New York: Henry Holt and Company, 1996.
Moss, Marissa. *Amelia's Notebook*. New York: Simon & Schuster Books for Young Readers, 1995.
Reynolds, Peter H. *Ish*. Cambridge, Mass.: Candlewick Press, 2004.
Spinelli, Eileen. *The Best Story Ever*. New York: Dial Books for Young Readers, 2008.
Tafuri, Nancy. *Have You Seen My Duckling?* New York: Greenwillow Books, 1984.
Williams, Sue. *I Went Walking*. San Diego: Red Wagon Books/Harcourt Inc., 1996.

WEB SITES

Book Making with Kids, www.bookmakingwithkids.com.
Susan Kapuscinski Gaylord's Making Books with Children, www.makingbooks.com.

MATERIALS

Cloth tape, www.paper-source.com

The Joy of Reading

Allen, Pam. *What to Read When*. New York: Avery, 2009.
Andrews, Julie, and Emma Walton Hamilton, eds. *Julie Andrews' Collection of Poems, Songs, and Lullabies*. New York: Little, Brown Books for Young Readers, 2009.
Banks, Kate. *Max's Words*. New York: Frances Foster Books, 2006.
Bear, Donald R., Marcia Invernizzi, Shane Templeton, and Francine Johnston. *Words Their Way: Word Study for Phonics, Vocabulary, and Spelling Instruction*. Upper Saddle River, New Jersey: Merrill, 2000.
Codell, Esmé Raji. *How to Get Your Child to Love Reading*. Chapel Hill: Algonquin Books of Chapel Hill, 2003.
Eccleshare, Julia, ed. *1001 Children's Books You Must Read before You Grow Up*. New York: Universe Publishing, 2009.
Ehlert, Lois. *Eating the Alphabet: Fruits and Vegetables from A to Z*. San Diego: Harcourt, 1989.
Falwell, Cathryn. *Word Wizard*. New York: Clarion Books, 1998.
Hamilton, Emma Walton. *Raising Bookworms*. Sag Harbor, New York: Beech Tree Books, 2009.
Harper, Charley. *ABCs*. Los Angeles: Ammo Books, 2008.
Harvey, Stephanie, and Anne Goudvis. *Strategies That Work*. New York: Stenhouse Publishers, 2000.
MacDonald, Suse. *Alphabatics*. New York: Simon & Schuster Books for Young Readers, 1986.
Martin Jr., Bill, and Michael Sampson, eds. *The Bill Martin Jr. Big Book of Poetry*. New York: Simon & Schuster Books for Young Readers, 2008.
McGuinness, Carmen, and Geoffrey McGuinness. *Reading Reflex*. New York: Fireside, 1998.
Metropolitan Museum of Art. *Museum ABC*. New York: Little, Brown and Company, 2002.
Munari, Bruno. *Bruno Munari's ABC*. San Francisco: Chronicle Books, 1960.
Nickle, John. *Alphabet Explosion: Search and Count from Alien to Zebra*. New York: Schwartz and Wade Books, 2006.
Pearle, Ida. *A Child's Day: An Alphabet of Play*. Orlando: Harcourt Inc., 2008.
Rand, Ann, and Paul Rand. *Sparkle and Spin: A Book about Words*. San Francisco: Chronicle Books, 2006.

Schotter, Roni. *The Boy Who Loved Words*. New York: Schwartz and Wade, 2006.

Werner, Sharon, and Sarah Forss. *Alphabeasties and Other Amazing Types*. Maplewood: Blue Apple Books, 2009.

Williams, Laura Ellen. *ABC Kids*. New York: Philomel Books, 2003.

Mathematicians at Work

Aber, Linda Williams. *Grandma's Button Box*. New York: The Kane Press, 2002.

Anno, Mitsumasa. *Anno's Counting Book*. New York: HarperCollins Publishers, 1975.

Baker, Keith. *Quack and Count*. San Diego: Harcourt Brace and Company, 1999.

Bang, Molly. *Ten, Nine, Eight*. New York: Greenwillow Books, 1983.

Baratta-Lorton, Mary. *Workjobs*. Parsippany, New Jersey : Dale Seymour Publications, 1972.

———. *Workjobs II*. Parsippany, New Jersey: Dale Seymour Publications, 1979.

Baylor, Byrd. *Everybody Needs a Rock*. New York: Atheneum Books for Young Readers, 1974.

Berkes, Marianne. *Over in the Ocean: In a Coral Reef*. Nevada City, Calif.: Dawn Publications, 2004.

———. *Seashells by the Seashore*. Nevada City, Calif.: Dawn Publications, 2002.

Burns, Marilyn. *About Teaching Mathematics: A K–8 Resource*. Sausalito, Calif.: Math Solutions Publications, 2000.

———. *Math and Literature (K–3) Book One*. Sausalito, Calif.: Math Solutions Publications, 1992.

Christian, Peggy. *If You Find a Rock*. San Diego: Harcourt, Inc., 2000.

Crews, Donald. *Ten Black Dots*. New York: Greenwillow Books, 1986.

Ehlert, Lois. *Fish Eyes: A Book You Can Count On*. San Diego: Harcourt Inc., 1990.

Giganti Jr., Paul. *Each Orange Had 8 Slices*. New York: Mulberry Books, 1992.

Keats, Jack Ezra. *Over in the Meadow*. New York: Viking, 1971.

Leedy, Loreen. *Measuring Penny*. New York: Henry Holt and Company, 1997.

Lionni, Leo. *Inch by Inch*. New York: HarperCollins Publishers, 1960.

———. *On My Beach There Are Many Pebbles*. New York: Astor-Honor Publishing, 1961.

Pilegard, Virginia Walton. *The Warlord's Beads*. Gretna: Pelican Publishing Company, Inc., 2001.

Pluckrose, Henry Arthur. *Pattern*. Chicago: Children's Press, 1995.

———. *Sorting*. London: Franklin Watts, 1988.

Reid, Margarette S. *The Button Box*. New York: Dutton Children's Books, 1990.

———. *A String of Beads*. New York: Dutton Children's Books, 1997.

Sturges, Philemon. *Ten Flashing Fireflies*. New York: North-South Books, 1995.

Sweeney, Joan. *Me and the Measure of Things*. New York: Crown Publishers, 2001.

Swinburne, Stephen R. *Lots and Lots of Zebra Stripes*. Pennsylvania: Boyd Mills Press, 1998.

Wadsworth, Olive A. *Over in the Meadow.* New York: Puffin Books, 1991.

Wormell, Christopher. *Teeth, Tails, and Tentacles: An Animal Counting Book.* New York: Scholastic Inc., 2005.

WEB SITES

The National Association for the Education of Young Children, 2002. www.naeyc .org/positionstatements/mathematics

Pattern Wizardry by the Brooklyn Children's Museum. www.brooklynkids.org/ patternwizardry

Scientific Investigations

Aloian, Molly, and Bobbie Kalman. *The Life Cycle of a Flower.* New York: Crabtree Publishing Company, 2004.

Aronson, Steven M. L. *Trees: North American Trees Identified by Leaf, Bark and Seed.* New York: Workman Publishing Company, 1997.

Banks, Kate. *And If the Moon Could Talk.* New York: Frances Foster Books, 1998.

Beachcomber's Guide to the North Atlantic Seashore. Lincoln, Mass.: Massachusetts Audubon Society, 1993.

Bearce, Stephanie. *A Kid's Guide to Making a Terrarium.* Hockessin, Del.: Mitchell Lane Publishers, 2010.

Bernard, Robin. *A Tree for All Seasons.* Washington D.C.: National Geographic Society, 1999.

Branley, Franklyn M. *Down Comes the Rain.* New York: HarperCollins Publishers, 1997.

———. *The Moon Seems to Change.* New York: Thomas Y. Crowell, 1987.

Burns, Diane L. *Trees, Leaves, and Bark.* Milwaukee: Gareth Stevens Publishing, 1998.

Carle, Eric. *Papa, Please Get the Moon for Me.* New York: Simon and Schuster, 1986.

Chambers, Catherine. *Bark.* Austin: Raintree Steck-Vaughn Publishers, 1996.

Chancer, Joni, and Gina Rester-Zodrow. *Moon Journals: Writing, Art, and Inquiry through Focused Nature Study.* Portsmouth, New Hampshire: Heinemann, 1997.

Cornell, Joseph. *Sharing Nature with Children.* Nevada City, New Jersey: Dawn Publications, 1979.

Curtis, Carolyn, and Allison Jay. *I Took the Moon for a Walk.* Cambridge, Mass.: Barefoot Books, 2004.

Day, John A. *The Book of Clouds.* New York: Sterling Publishing Co., 2005.

Day, John A., and Vincent J. Schaefer. *Peterson First Guides: Clouds and Weather.* Boston: Houghton Mifflin, 1991.

dePaola, Tomie. *The Cloud Book.* New York: Holiday House, 1975.

Fletcher, Ralph. *Hello, Harvest Moon.* New York: Clarion Books, 2003.

Fowler, Allan. *From Seed to Plant.* New York: Grolier Publishing, 2001.

Gibbons, Gail. *The Moon Book.* New York: Holiday House, 1997.

————. *The Seasons of Arnold's Apple Tree*. San Diego: Harcourt Brace Jovanovich, 1984.

————. *From Seed to Plant*. New York: Holiday House, 1991.

————. *Tell Me, Tree: All about Trees for Kids*. Boston: Little, Brown and Company, 2002.

Heller, Ruth. *The Reason for a Flower*. New York: Scholastic, 1983.

Hosoume, Kimi, and Jacqueline Barber. *Terrarium Habitats Teacher's Guide*. Berkeley: Great Explorations in Math and Science, Lawrence Hall of Science, University of California Berkeley, 1994.

Ingoglia, Gina. *The Tree Book for Kids and Their Grown Ups*. Brooklyn: Brooklyn Botanic Garden, 2008.

Jeunesse, Gallimard, Elisabeth Cohat, and Pierre De Hugo. *The Seashore*. New York: Scholastic, 1990.

Kricher, John C. *Peterson First Guides: Seashores*. Boston: Houghton Mifflin Company, 1992.

Lauber, Patricia. *Be a Friend to Trees*. New York: HarperCollins Publishers, 1994.

Locker, Thomas. *Sky Tree: Seeing Science through Art*. New York: HarperCollins Publishers, 1995.

————. *Water Dance*. San Diego: Harcourt Brace and Company, 1997.

McKinney, Barbara Shaw. *A Drop around the World*. Nevada City, New Jersey: Dawn Publications, 1998.

Pascoe, Elaine. *The Ecosystem of an Apple Tree*. New York: PowerKids Press, 2003.

Pelo, Ann. *The Language of Art*. St. Paul, Minn.: Redleaf Press, 2007.

Prager, Ellen J. *Sand*. Washington, D.C.: National Geographic, 2000.

Pretor-Pinney, Gavin. *The Cloudspotter's Guide: The Science, History, and Culture of Clouds*. New York: The Berkley Publishing Group, 2006.

Reed-Jones, Carol. *The Tree in the Ancient Forest*. Nevada City, New Jersey: Dawn Publications, 1995.

Robbins, Ken. *Seeds*. New York: Atheneum Books for Young Readers, 2005.

Rockwell, Anne. *One Bean*. New York: Walker and Company, 1998.

Rosinsky, Natalie. *Dirt: The Scoop on Soil*. Minneapolis: Picture Window Books, 2003.

Schaefer, Lola M. *Pick, Pull, Snap! Where Once a Flower Bloomed*. New York: Greenwillow Books, 2003.

Seymour, Arlene. *The Moon Book: A Lunar Pop-Up Celebration*. New York: Universe Publishing, 2003.

Shaw, Charles G. *It Looked Like Spilt Milk*. New York: HarperCollins Publishers, 1947.

Silver, Donald M. *One Small Square: Seashore*. New York: Learning Triangle Press, 1993.

Strauss, Rochelle. *One Well: The Story of Water on Earth*. Tonawanda, New York: Kids Can Press, 2007.

Thurber, James. *Many Moons*. San Diego: Harcourt Brace Jovanovich, 1998.

Tomecek, Steve. *Dirt*. Washington, D.C.: National Geographic, 2002.

Trail, Gayla. *Grow Great Grub: Organic Food from Small Places*. New York: Clarkson Potter, 2010.

Udry, Janice May. *A Tree Is Nice*. New York: HarperCollins Publishers, 1956.

Vitale, Alice Thoms. *Leaves in Myth, Magic and Medicine*. New York: Stewart, Tabori & Chang, 1997.

Wallace, Nancy Elizabeth. *Seeds! Seeds! Seeds!* Tarrytown, New York: Marshall Cavendish Children, 2007.

Wick, Walter. *A Drop of Water: A Book of Science and Wonder*. New York: Scholastic Press, 1997.

Yolen, Jane. *Owl Moon*. New York: Philomel Books, 1987.

Zolotow, Charlotte. *The Moon Was the Best*. New York: Greenwillow Books, 1993.

Zim, Herbert S., and Lester Ingle. *Seashore Life: A Guide to Animals and Plants Along the Beach*. New York: St. Martin's Press, 1955.

WEB SITES

The Old Farmer's Almanac, www.almanac.com/moon

Steven M. Lewers and Associates Folding Guides, www.foldingguides.com

Exploring Art and Artists

Anholt, Laurence. *The Magical Garden of Claude Monet*. Hauppauge, New York: Barron's Educational Series, Inc., 2003.

———. *Matisse: The King of Color*. Hauppauge: Barron's Educational Series, Inc., 2007.

Bell, Julian. *Five Hundred Self-Portraits*. London: Phaidon, 2000.

Bennett, Leonie. *The Life and Work of . . . Jackson Pollock*. Chicago: Heinemann Library, 2005.

Brookes, Mona. *Drawing with Children: A Creative Teaching and Learning Method That Works for Adults Too*. New York: G.P. Putnam's Sons, 1986.

Collins, Pat Lowery. *I Am an Artist*. Minneapolis: Millbrook Press, 1992.

Cowart, Jack, et al. *Henri Matisse Paper Cut-Outs*. New York: Harry N. Abrams Inc., 1977.

Edwards, Pamela Duncan. *The Neat Line: Scribbling through Mother Goose*. New York: Katherine Tegen Books, 2005.

Ehlert, Lois. *Hands: Growing Up to Be an Artist*. San Diego: Harcourt, Inc., 1997.

Eldredge, Charles C. *Georgia O'Keeffe: American and Modern*. New York: Harry N. Abrams Inc., 1991.

Falconer, Ian. *Olivia*. New York: Atheneum/Anne Schwartz Books, 2000.

Frank, Elizabeth. *Pollock*. New York: Abbeville Press Publishers, 1983.

Gardner, Howard. *Art Education and Human Development*. Los Angeles: The J. Paul Getty Museum, 1990.

Greenberg, Jan, and Sandra Jordan. *Action Jackson*. Brookfield: Roaring Book Press, 2002.

Johnson, Keesia, and Jane O'Connor. *Henri Matisse: Drawing with Scissors*. New York: Grosset and Dunlap, 2002.

Katz, Karen. *The Colors of Us*. New York: Henry Holt and Company, 1999.

Kohl, Maryann F., and Jean Potter. *Storybook Art*. Bellingham, Wash.: Bright Ring Publishing, Inc., 2003.

Lasky, Kathryn. *Georgia Rises: A Day in the Life of Georgia O'Keeffe*. New York: Melanie Kroupa Books, 2009.

Leslie, Clare Walker, and Charles E. Roth. *Keeping a Nature Journal: Discover a Whole New Way of Seeing the World around You*. North Adams, Mass.: Storey Publishing, 2003.

Le Tord, Bijou. *A Blue Butterfly: A Story about Claude Monet*. New York: Delacorte Press, 1995.

Ljungkvist, Laura. *Follow the Line around the World*. New York: Viking, 2008.

Mobility of Expression. Municipality of Reggio Emilia Infant-Toddler Centers and Preschools. Reggio Emilia: Reggio Children, 1995. http://zerosei.comune.re.it/inter/pubs/portfolios.htm.

Moulin, Raoul Jean. *Henri Matisse: Drawings and Paper Cut-Outs*. New York: McGraw Hill Book Company, 1969.

Packard, Steven. *Claude Monet: Sunshine and Waterlilies*. New York: Grosset and Dunlap, 2001.

Pelo, Ann. *The Language of Art*. St. Paul, Minn.: Redleaf Press, 2007.

Prévert, Jacques. *How to Paint the Portrait of a Bird*. New York: Roaring Book Press, 2007.

Reynolds, Peter H. *The Dot*. Somerville, Mass.: Candlewick Press, 2003.

———. *Ish*. Somerville: Candlewick Press, 2004.

Rodriguez, Rachel. *Through Georgia's Eyes*. New York: Henry Holt and Company, 2006.

Rohmer, Harriet, ed. *Just Like Me: Stories and Self-Portraits by Fourteen Artists*. San Francisco: Children's Book Press, 1997.

Sabbeth, Carol. *Monet and the Impressionists for Kids*. Chicago: Chicago Review Press, 2002.

Smith, Nancy R. *Experience and Art*. New York: Teachers College Press, 1993.

Turner, Robyn Montana. *Georgia O'Keeffe: Portraits of Women Artists for Children*. Boston: Little, Brown and Company, 1991.

Venezia, Mike. *Georgia O'Keeffe*. Chicago: Children's Press, 1993.

———. *Henri Matisse*. Chicago: Children's Press, 1997.

Whitman, Candace. *Lines That Wiggle*. Maplewood, New Jersey: Blue Apple Books, 2009.

Winter, Jeanette. *My Name Is Georgia*. San Diego: Silver Whistle, 1998.

Yenawine, Philip. *Lines*. New York: Museum of Modern Art, Delacorte Press, 1991.

MATERIALS

For more interactive questions that enhance a child's experience of and interaction with artwork, I highly recommend MUSE QUESTS (Questions for Understanding, Exploring, Seeing and Thinking). These small self-guided booklets are available through Project Zero Publications (http://pzpublications.com/12.html).

Growing Globally

A Life Like Mine. New York: Dorling Kindersley Publishing in Association with UNICEF, 2002.

A School Like Mine. New York: Dorling Kindersley Publishing in Association with UNICEF, 2007.

Aberg, Rebecca. *Latitude and Longitude*. New York: Children's Press, 2003.

Ahlberg, Allan. *Treasure Hunt*. Cambridge, Mass.: Candlewick Press, 2002.

Arthus-Bertrand, Yann. *Earth from Above*. New York: Harry N. Abrams, Inc., 2002.

Bednar, Sylvie. *Flags of the World*. New York: Abrams Books for Young Readers, 2009.

Beeler, Selby B. *Throw Your Tooth on the Roof: Tooth Traditions from around the World*. Boston: Houghton Mifflin Company, 1998.

Beginner's World Atlas. Washington D.C.: National Geographic, 2005.

Caseley, Judith. *On the Town*. New York: Greenwillow Books, 2002.

Chesanow, Neil. *Where Do I Live?* Hauppauge, New York: Barron's, 1995.

D'Aluisio, Faith, and Peter Mnezel. *Hungry Planet: What the World Eats*. Berkeley: Material World Books and Ten Speed Press, 2005.

Fanelli, Sara. *My Map Book*. New York: HarperCollins Publishers, 1995.

Harshman, Marc, and Barbara Garrison. *Only One Neighborhood*. New York: Dutton Children's Books, 2007.

Hollyer, Beatrice. *Wake Up, World! A Day in the Life of Children around the World*. New York: Henry Holt and Company in Association with Oxfam, 1999.

Howard, Rebecca. *Flagtastic Flags*. London: Marion Boyars Publishers Ltd., 2006.

Jenkins, Steve. *Hottest Coldest Highest Deepest*. Boston: Houghton Mifflin Company, 1998.

Komatsu, Yoshio. *Wonderful Houses around the World*. Bolinas, Calif.: Shelter Publications, 2004.

Leedy, Loreen. *Mapping Penny's World*. New York: Henry Holt and Company, 2000.

Mara, Wil. *The Seven Continents*. New York: Children's Press, 2005.

Marzollo, Jean. *I Spy Treasure Hunt: A Book of Picture Riddles*. New York: Scholastic, 1999.

Morris, Ann. *Families*. New York: Lothrop, Lee and Shepard Books, 2000.

———. *Houses and Homes*. New York: Lothrop, Lee and Shepard Books, 1995.

———. *Loving*. New York: Lothrop, Lee and Shepard Books, 1990.

———. *Play*. New York: Lothrop, Lee and Shepard Books, 1998.

————. *Teamwork*. New York: Lothrop, Lee and Shepard Books, 1999.

Menzel, Peter. *Material World: A Global Family Portrait*. San Francisco: Sierra Club Books, 1994.

Murphy, Stuart J. *Treasure Map*. New York: HarperCollins Publishers, 2004.

Reynolds, Jan. *Celebrate! Connections among Cultures*. New York: Lee and Low Books Inc., 2006.

Ritchie, Scot. *Follow That Map! A First Book of Mapping Skills*. Tonawanda, New York: Kids Can Press, 2009.

Schuett, Stacey. *Somewhere in the World Right Now*. New York: Alfred A. Knopf, 1995.

Shaskan, Trisha Speed. *The Treasure Map*. Minneapolis: Picture Window Books, 2007.

Smithsonion Handbooks, *Complete Flags of the World*. New York: DK Publishing, 2008.

Sobel, David. *Mapmaking with Children*. Portsmouth, New Hampshire: Heinemann, 1949.

Stojic, Manya. *Hello World: Greetings in 42 Languages around the Globe!* New York: Scholastic, 2002.

Suárez-Orozco, Marcelo M., and Desirée Baolian Qin-Hilliard, eds. *Globalization: Culture and Education in the New Millennium*. Berkeley: University of California Press and Ross Institute, 2004.

Swain, Gwenyth. *Bedtime!* Minneapolis: First Ave. Editions, 2002.

————. *Get Dressed!* Minneapolis: First Ave. Editions, 2002.

————. *Tidy Up!* Minneapolis: First Ave. Editions, 2002.

Sweeney, Joan. *Me on the Map*. New York: Crown Publishers, Inc., 1996.

Taylor, Barbara. *Maps and Mapping*. New York: Kingfisher Books, 1992.

Thong, Roseanne. *Wish: Wishing Traditions around the World*. San Francisco: Chronicle Books, 2008.

WEB SITES

Central Intelligence Agency, https://www.cia.gov/library/publications/the-world-factbook/docs/flagsoftheworld.html

Colouring Book of Flags, http://flagspot.net/flags/cbk.html

The Crafty Crow: A Children's Craft Collective, http://belladia.typepad.com/crafty_crow/crafts-around-the-world

Raising the Citizens of Tomorrow

Aardema, Verna. *Why Mosquitoes Buzz in People's Ears*. New York: Dial Books for Young Readers, 1975.

Alexander, Lloyd. *The Fortune-Tellers*. New York: Dutton Children's Books, 1992.

Aliki. *Feelings*. New York: Mulberry Books, 1986.

Bourgeois, Paulette. *Franklin Is Bossy*. New York: Scholastic, 1993.

Brandenberg, Aliki. *Feelings.* New York: Greenwillow Books, 1984.

Breeding, Ken, and Harrison, Jane. *Connected and Respected.* Cambridge, Mass.: Educators for Social Responsibility, 2007.

Bunting, Eve. *Fly Away Home.* New York: Clarion Books, 1991.

Cooney, Barbara. *Miss Rumphius.* New York: The Viking Press, 1982.

Curtis, Jamie Lee. *Today I Feel Silly: And Other Moods That Make My Day.* New York: Joanna Cotler Books, 1998.

Dr. Seuss. *My Many Colored Days.* New York: Alfred A. Knopf, 1996.

Estes, Eleanor. *The Hundred Dresses.* Orlando, Florida: Harcourt, 2004.

Grimes, Nikki. *Oh, Bother! Someone's Fighting.* New York: A Golden Book, 1991.

Henkes, Kevin. *Chrysanthemum.* New York: Greenwillow Books, 1991.

Katz, Karen. *Can You Say Peace?* New York: Henry Holt and Company, 2006.

Kerley, Barbara. *A Little Peace.* Washington, D.C.: National Geographic, 2007.

Krischanitz, Raoul. *Nobody Likes Me!* New York: North-South Books, 1999.

Lantiera, Linda. *Techniques to Cultivate Inner Strength in Children: Building Emotional Intelligence.* Boulder: Sounds True, 2008.

Lewis, Barbara A. *The Kid's Guide to Service Projects: Over 500 Service Ideas for Young People Who Want to Make a Difference.* Minneapolis: Free Spirit Publishing Inc, 1995.

Lewis, Kim. *Friends.* Cambridge, Mass.: Candlewick Press, 1997.

MacLean, Kerry Lee. *Peaceful Piggy Meditation.* Morton Grove, Ill.: Albert Whitman and Company, 2004.

Menzel, Peter. *Material World: A Global Family Portrait.* San Francisco: Sierra Club Books, 1994.

Parr, Todd. *The Peace Book.* New York: Little, Brown and Company, 2004.

Radunsky, Vladimir, and Children from around the World. *What Does Peace Feel Like?* New York: Atheneum Books for Young Readers, 2004.

Reider, Katja, and Angela von Roehl. *Snail Started It!* New York: North-South Books, 1997.

Rice, Judith Anne. *The Kindness Curriculum: Introducing Young Children to Loving Values.* St. Paul, Minn.: Redleaf Press, 1995.

Shepard, Aaron. *Forty Fortunes: A Tale of Iran.* New York: Clarion Books, 1999.

Snow, Todd and Peggy. *Feelings to Share from A to Z.* Oak Park Heights, Minn.: Maren Green Publishing, Inc., 2007.

Thomas, Shelley Moore. *Somewhere Today: A Book of Peace.* Park Ridge, Ill.: Albert Whitman and Company, 1998.

Wood, Audrey. *Quick as a Cricket.* Swindon, England: Child's Play (International) Ltd., 1982.

Wood, Douglas. *Making the World.* New York: Simon and Schuster Books for Young Readers, 1998.

———. *A Quiet Place.* New York: Simon and Schuster Books for Young Readers, 2002.

Zolotow, Charlotte. *The Quarreling Book*. New York: Harper and Row Publishers, 1963.
Zeiler, Freddi. *A Kid's Guide to Giving*. Norwalk, Conn: innovativeKids, 2006.

WEB SITES

American Institute of Philanthropy, www.charitywatch.org/toprated.html
Arbor Day Foundation, www.arborday.org/programs/volunteers/States.cfm
Charity Navigator, www.charitynavigator.org/
The Collaborative for Academic, Social, and Emotional Learning, www.casel.org
DonorsChoose.org, www.donorschoose.org
Feeding America, http://feedingamerica.org/foodbank-results.aspx
First Book, www.firstbook.org
Goodwill, http://locator.goodwill.org/
Heifer International, www.heifer.org
Kiva, www.kiva.org
Meals on Wheels, www.mowaa.org/Page.aspx?pid=262
National Park Service, www.nps.gov/getinvolved/volunteer.htm
Roots and Shoots, www.rootsandshoots.org/kidsandteens
Smart Givers Network, www.smartgivers.org/
United States House of Representatives, https://writerep.house.gov/writerep/
    welcome.shtml
United States Senate, www.senate.gov/general/contact_information/senators_cfm
    .cfm
The White House, www.whitehouse.gov/contact

Index

About the Author

MARIAH BRUEHL is an educator at heart. After receiving her master's degree in elementary education from Bank Street College, she taught at the Dalton School in New York. She then became the associate director of the Ross Lower School in Bridgehampton, New York.

After years of working in the field of education, Mariah made the decision to dedicate more time to her two young daughters. Among the many benefits of their time together was the birth of her award-winning Web site, Playful Learning, which was created to help parents support their children's learning and development.

Mariah lives with her husband and two children in Long Island, New York. She can also be found teaching classes to parents, teachers, and children in her storefront and workshop space in Sag Harbor, also called Playful Learning.